Gluten Free for the 5:2 Fast Diet

All the Recipes You Need to Lose Weight Fast

by Liz Armond

Published in UK by:
Liz Armond

© Copyright 2014 – Liz Armond

ISBN-13: 978-1512252491
ISBN-10: 1512252492

ALL RIGHTS RESERVED. No part of this publication may be reproduced or transmitted in any form whatsoever, electronic, or mechanical, including photocopying, recording, or by any informational storage or retrieval system without express written, dated and signed permission from the author.

Table of Contents

Introduction 1
The 5:2 Fasting Diet 3
Diet the Healthy Way 7
Who Should <u>NOT</u> Fast? 9
Why Gluten Free? 11
Some Essential Cookery Notes 13
BREAKFASTS 19
    Some More Simple Breakfasts 21
    Kippers 21
    Porridge with Various 22
    Scrambled Eggs with Various Fillings 23
    Fruit Platter 24
    Fruit Fool 24
    Egg White Omelette 25
    Low Calorie Fried Breakfast 26
    Another Fry Up 27

  EASY LUNCHES 28
    Bacon Lettuce & Tomato Sandwich 28
    Cottage Cheese on Various 29
    Poached Eggs with Spinach 30
    Potato Salad 31

  LESS THAN 200 CALORIES 33
  VEGETARIAN 34
    Butternut Squash Soup – 150 kcal 34
    Cauliflower Crumb Bake - 120 kcal 36
    Easy Mixed Salad - 40 kcal 38
    Hearty Potato & Leek Soup – 150 kcal 40
    Hungarian Vegetables - 115 kcal 42

 Lentil & Spring Greens Soup – 110 kcal 46
 Low Calorie Hummus – 125 kcal................................ 48
 Mini Cheese Soufflé - 150 kcal..................................... 50
 Mixed Salad with Avocado – 120 kcal....................... 52
 Moroccan Spicy Tofu - 195 calories........................... 54
 Pea and Spinach Dahl – 160 kcal................................ 56
 Ratatouille – 105 kcal 58
 Spicy Veggie Burgers - 170 kcal.................................. 60
 Thai Split Pea & Carrot Soup - 125 kcal.................... 62
 Tomato & Courgette Bake - 185 kcal........................ 64
 Tomato and Red Pepper Soup – 95 kcal................... 66
 Tzatsiki – 50 kcal 68
 Vegetable and Citrus Soup - 80 kcal 70
 Vegetable Curry – 180 kcal... 72

FISH 74
 Canned Tuna Salad – 146 kcal.................................... 74
 Mussels in Tasty Sauce – 185 kcal............................. 75
 Prawn and Fennel Soup – 110 kcal 78
 Tuna and White Bean Salad – 160 kcal.................... 80
 Cabbage & Prawns – 180 kcal 82

MEAT & POULTRY 84
 Chicken Tarragon & Lemon – 175 kcal..................... 84
 Curry Coated Chicken – 176 kcal 86
 Pork and Apple Medallions -192 kcal 90
 Pork with Pine Nuts – 200 kcal.................................. 92
 Turkey and Vegetable Loaf – 180 kcal...................... 94
 Vegetable & Meat Soup – 180 kcal............................ 96

LESS THAN 300 CALORIES.. 99
VEGETARIAN 100
 Chilli Beans - 200 kcal.. 100

Five Bean Wrap – 294 kcal 102
Hearty Summer Salad – 294 kcal 104
Leek & Bean Frittata - 215 kcal 106
Mushroom Omelette & Salad – 255 kcal 108
Mushroom Risotto – 284 kcal 110
Nutty Mushroom Pilaf - 298 kcal 112
Spicy Potato Wraps – 235 kcal 114
Spinach & Mushroom Stew - 210 kcal 116
Sweet Potato Curry Wraps - 280 kcal 118
Vegetable & Bean Stew – 270 kcal 120

FISH 122

Baked Curried Cod – 246 kcal 122
Fishcakes & Tomato Sauce – 290 kcal 124
Mussels in White Wine – 278 kcal 126
Prawn and Chilli Wrap – 240 kcal 128
Prawn and Dill Soup – 250 kcal 130
Tuna & Salmon Kebabs – 355 kcal 132
Salmon & Ginger Stir Fry – 295 kcal 134
Tuna Curry Broth 239 kcal 136
Tuna Steaks &Beans – 250 kcal 138

MEAT & POULTRY 140

Beef Strips with Pak Choy – 265 kcal 140
Beef with Green Lentils – 220 kcal 142
Chicken & Cherry Tomatoes – 260 kcal 146
Chicken Parcels – 280 kcal 148
Chicken & Cabbage Broth – 250 kcal 150
Lamb and Apricot Casserole – 280 kcal 154
Pork Chilli with Beans – 294 kcal 156
Pork & Mixed Peppers – 285 kcal 158
Pork & Roasted Vegetables – 235 kcal 160

Spicy Chicken Pitta – 275 kcal 162

LESS THAN 400 CALORIES 165
VEGETARIAN 166
    Baked Veggie Pasta - 385 kcal 166
    Butternut Squash Risotto – 365 kcal 168
    Fresh Pesto with Pasta – 365 kcal 170
    Golden Rice & Red Onions – 365 kcal 172
    Leek and Mushroom Bake - 330 kcal 176
    Low Fat Pesto Tagliatelle – 350 kcal 178
    Mixed Vegetable Bake – 330 kcal 180
    Mushroom Risotto – 365 kcal 182
    Mushrooms & Mustard Mash - 390 kcal 184
    Pasta with Cherry Tomatoes - 325 kcal 186
    Penne with Pepper Sauce – 375 kcal 188
    Sweetcorn Soufflé - 325 kcal 190
    Tofu with Noodles - 385 kcal 192
    Vegetable Stew & Dumplings - 315 kcal 194
    Vegetable & Tofu Stew - 345 kcal 196
    Vegetarian Chilli – 390 kcal 198
    Sweet Potato Curry – 350 kcal 200

FISH 202
    Fruity Fish Kebabs – 335 kcal 202
    Olive and Anchovy Pasta – 365 kcal 204
    Tuna Steak & Mash – 325 kcal 206
    Tuna Steak & Vegetables – 385 kcal 208

MEAT & POULTRY 210
    Beef and Courgette Bake – 320 kcal 210
    Chicken Lasagne – 390 kcal 214
    Chicken and Chips – 400 kcal 216
    Italian Turkey Steak – 325 kcal 220

Honey Chicken with Pasta – 365 kcal 222
Lamb Kebabs - 325 kcal 224
Sausages in Batter - 325 kcal 226
Marinated Balsamic Beef – 330 kcal 228
Pork and Plum Hotpot – 350 kcal 230
Pork Stroganoff with Rice – 330 kcal 232
Tomato &Chicken with Pasta 340 kcal 234

About the Author 236
One Final Thing 237
Books by Liz Armond 238
DISCLAIMER AND/OR LEGAL NOTICES: 239

Introduction

This cookbook has been specially adapted to use gluten-free ingredients in all the recipes. This will help you plan your low calorie meals if you are using the 5:2 Fast Diet to lose weight but are also gluten intolerant or Celiac.

I started intermittent fasting a couple of years ago as a simple way to lose some excess weight as well as help me to live a healthier and hopefully longer life. I then wrote a book called Fasting Your Way to Health in which I included a chapter on the relatively new 5:2 Fast Diet because it had become one of the most popular diets around.

I have since written a series of cookbooks for this diet which are listed at the end of this cookbook. All of them aim to solve your problem on what to eat on your 2 fasting days without having to cook fancy and expensive food which many of the other 5.2 cookbooks seem to do.

I have family and friends who are also Gluten intolerant (Coeliac/Celiac) and they wanted to try the 2 day diet but couldn't be 100% sure the recipe ingredients were suitable for their gluten-free diets. So in this and my Vegetarian and Gluten-Free Cookbook I have adapted many of my standard recipes to suit them as well as adding a few others into the mix.

Finding gluten free products and ingredients should not be a chore as a huge range is available in most big supermarkets and food stores. In the UK, health stores like Holland & Barrett stock many of the specialised gluten-free products and there are plenty of other health shops that stock the same. You can also get almost everything you need online.

However, as you look through this cookbook you will realise that you already have a lot of the basics in your store cupboard and even if you don't the few you will have to buy are not expensive and can be used for other recipes again and again. You won't be buying spices etc. to use for just one dish.

Many of the recipes you can have for lunch or dinner, although the breakfasts are a little different in that they are mostly very low calorie so would probably not suit lunch or dinner, but of course that's up to you, you may love porridge for tea.

Above everything, enjoy your food and remember it is only for 2 days a week, you don't need to think about dieting for the other 5 days, although you will find you are taking notice of labelling and calories much more than you used to.

The 5:2 Fasting Diet

The 5:2 diet or Fast Diet or Intermittent Diet are just a few names given to a very popular proven way of losing weight, so called because generally speaking you can eat as you would normally (within reason) on 5 days a week but on the other 2 days, known as fasting days you must restrict your food and drink intake to only 500 calories if you are female or 600 calories if you are a male. This is regardless of your current weight or how much you need to lose.

It doesn't matter which days you choose to feed or fast but it is recommended that the fasting days are not done together. Depending on the speed you wish to lose the weight you could adjust the ratio of fasting to feeding days. For example you could try a 6:1 or 5:2 or 4:3 and so on. When you have reached your ideal weight perhaps then is the time to only fast for one day a week to maintain your target weight, but for now let's assume you have a goal to reach, so we will a look at the normal 5:2

diet in more depth.

On fasting days you can elect to consume all of your calories in one go, or more usual to spread them throughout the day. Breakfast can either be a really low calorie count which means you can probably have a light lunch as well or you can skip it altogether. I found skipping breakfast worked better for me as it didn't kick start my juices first thing and I had no problem lasting until midday lunch.

I quite often forgot all about food and went to 1 or 2 o'clock before I realised I was getting hungry. I don't think I could eat breakfast and then have nothing until my evening meal unless I was seriously fasting, meaning I was going without all food for that day. I cover this in more depth in my book **Fasting Your Way to Health**

There is varying opinion on whether filling up at breakfast or snacking throughout the day is more effective for weight loss. You will find your own preferred method, I tried both and found that splitting my calories between lunch and dinner worked better for me but then I can manage to skip breakfast but you may not be able to.

Drink plenty of water or tea or coffee to fill your empty stomach but no sugar and watch your milk intake or you will be eating into your calories. Having said that, please don't worry too much about going a little over the 500 calories bit because when you follow this eating plan you will be amazed at how you start to look at everything you eat on your 'normal' days and will in fact eat less over the 7 days anyway.

On your 5 normal days you can eat whatever you like within reason. This is not carte blanch to load your system with unhealthy junk food. What you will find is that you are looking at packaging much more than you used to.

You will be shocked at the amount of calories in one chocolate biscuit, I know I was. If you think about the calories in that one biscuit and then think of the percentage that biscuit is of your 500 or 600 calorie allowance on your fasting days you quickly come to appreciate why that weight gain crept on in the first place.

Remember if the hunger pangs become too much, do something active like going for a walk. You can drink as much water as you like and this will fill you up too. Try a little honey or lemon juice in a glass of warm water, you will soon feel full until your meal is due.

If you are doing this with your partner, don't forget to factor in an additional 100 calories if either of you is male.

If you are worried about the long term effects on your body, contrary to what some people think, fasting can be a healthy way to lose weight. It can reduce levels of IGF-1 (insulin-like growth factor 1, which can lead to accelerated ageing). It can also 'switch' on DNA repair genes as well as reducing blood pressure and lowering cholesterol and glucose levels.

A word of warning, it is not recommended for pregnant women or diabetics on medication. In fact anyone who has health problems or has an existing medical condition is strongly advised to consult their GP first. This is not to say you can't follow this diet, it is just so you can clear it with your Doctor in case you should do it under medical advice or supervision.

Finally, keep going by thinking to yourself that this is only for 2 days a week, you are not on a full blown 7 days a week diet for weeks on end or in some cases what seems like forever.

Well that's all there is to it, well almost. As I said before if you are interested in other methods of fasting, I cover this in my book on losing weight and getting healthier through fasting called, **Fasting Your Way to Health**

Diet the Healthy Way

So, how do you diet the healthy way?

Be accountable.

Whatever the consequences are, you need to be accountable for your actions and diet for the right reasons. Likewise, be sensitive to the response or reaction of family and friends who you confide in about your plans to reduce you food intake for 2 days a week. It is likely that they might have seen something detrimental in the press or on television about the dangers of not eating normally and will only be showing concern for you and your wellbeing.

Prepare in advance.

When you have come to the decision to start any type of diet, do not act on the spur of the moment, it will work much better if you have done your preparation beforehand. Make sure you know what appointments or events are likely to happen before, during and after your fasting days. You don't want to plan a fasting day only to find you had forgotten you were having lunch with your best friend or had booked a game of golf. If you don't skimp on the preparation time, your fasting day will most likely go more smoothly and be much more enjoyable and effective. Try to do the same days each week, it helps set the mind into a routine.

Understand the effects on your body.

If you have managed to read some facts and figures on fasting you will know that your body goes through several distinct phases when you begin to fast. It is possible that during the first few hours, you will feel a little weak, especially if you have decided to go without breakfast. You shouldn't be too alarmed by this as it is natural as your body begins to eliminate the toxins in your system.

Break the fast properly.

If you are planning to do the 5:2 fast, you won't have many serious side effects but it doesn't hurt to be prepared. Try not to have a great big fry up the next day as a form of reward. Have your usual cereal so you don't waste your previous day of good eating.

Who Should **NOT** Fast?

The 5:2 fast will have very little adverse effect on many of the following groups, but use your common sense

1. Infants and children. There is really no good reason for infants and children to fast. Due to their lack of maturity, they would likely not really understand the spiritual purpose of fasting, and their growing bodies need to take in ample nutrients regularly.

2. Pregnant or nursing women. Most fasts, including the 5:2 should be avoided by women who are pregnant or nursing unless cleared by a Doctor. The baby requires so many nutrients for normal development and is dependent on the mother's proper nutrition to receive those nutrients. You are forcing the unborn baby to fast and can be potentially dangerous to both mother and child.

3. People with Cancer - Do not fast unless you are fasting in an attempt to help yourself heal in which case this should be under direct medical advice. The 5:2 is probably not severe enough for this purpose. Cancer is usually indicative of, amongst other things, an immune system that is not in good shape.

4. People with other health concerns. The 5:2 Fast Diet is a good way to regulate food intake on overweight or obese sufferers and juice fasts may be another option. However check with your Doctor first as he may wish to supervise your weight loss.

5. The Elderly - There is no need for the elderly to fast as their body may not be able to manage such a task but it may not hurt them to lose a little weight for mobility reasons. Again use your common sense and perhaps only try 1 day intermittent fasting to start.

And if anyone still has any concerns or questions, they should always ask their doctor. Remember, fasting is supposed to help bring out the best of health for us.

Why Gluten Free?

The clue is in the name, Gluten and if you mentally associate gluten with glue that is exactly what it is. Next time you have a slice of crusty bread or delicious chicken pie, imagine them sticking straight to your hips or bottom because that's what gluten does when contained in the foods you eat.

Gluten is a protein contained in the endosperm of the wheat plant and it is added to a wide variety of foods to bind them together or to make them perform better.

The wheat plant is ground up into a fine powder which we call flour and this is traditionaly made into breads, pastas, and many other products we routinely buy.

When you first try to cut out gluten you will not have all the ingredients to hand so here are a few substutions that will help you follow a gluten-free diet.

Baking powder

Use ½ tsp. of cream of tartar and ¼ tsp. baking soda to replace your baking powder.

Flour

Use cornflour or corn starch in place of ordinary flour. This will work just as well for thickening or for texture.

Buttermilk

For any recipe that calls for buttermilk, just use soya milk and add a tablespoon of lemon juice per 225ml/8 fl oz / 1 cup. If you don't have soya milk you can use a plain gluten-free yoghurt to make up the same quantities.

Chocolate

If you would rather not use chocolate, mix together a tablespoon of oil and 2 tablespoons of cocoa powder and use instead. This is a preferred substitution for many on a gluten-free diet because of the nicer taste.

Milk

Use Soy or almond or coconut milk in place of ordinary milk if you are on a gluten free diet.

Balsamic Vinegar

This is usually gluten free but if using a cheaper version check the label to make sure they haven't bulked it up with anything.

Some Essential Cookery Notes

The main recipes in this book are suitable for either lunches or dinners, depending on how you have decided to split your allowance on the fasting days. They are all tried and tested and I have attempted to give the menu for 1 serving where possible. Where this has proved difficult because of the ingredient quantities they will be for 2 or 4 servings.

If I have given ½ a can of beans or other split ingredients the remainder can be stored in the fridge or freezer for other recipes or used for a non fasting day meal. This has not been a problem for me because my husband is also fasting so I cook either 2 portions or 4 portions and freeze the excess. This is very handy when you want a quick lunch or dinner on your fasting days.

I do recommend that you cook as big a portion as possible, that way you always have a meal in the freezer or fridge. Let's face it; it will be easier on your fasting days if you are not surrounded by food waiting to be cooked.

The ingredients in this book are given in the standard UK measurements and the metric equivalent and where I have been able to I have also given the US equivalent. You should choose one of them but do not mix. Where I have not given appropriate quantities you can convert them using the easy table below.

Recipes use many different abbreviations. Here are some I have used in this book.

Standard UK/US

tsp = teaspoon
tbsp = tablespoon
oz/s = ounce/ s
lb/s = pound/s
fl. oz. = fluid ounce

Metric

ml = millilitres
ltr = liter/litre
g = grams

Weights & Volumes

Cup measurements which are widely used in the US and Australia are difficult to list because they vary according to what you are weighing. You should weigh out your dry ingredients using kitchen scales

Teaspoons and tablespoons are level measure.

1 tsp = 5ml
1 tbsp = 15ml

Liquid conversions

1 tsp = 5 ml
1 tbsp = 3 tsp = 15 ml

metric	imperial	US
50ml	2 fl oz	¼ cup
125ml	4 fl oz	½ cup
175ml	6 fl oz	¾ cup
225ml	8 fl oz	1 cup
300ml	10 fl oz / ½ pint	1¼ cups
450ml	16 fl oz	2 cups / 1 pint
600ml	20 fl oz / 1 pint	2½ cups
1 litre	35 fl oz / 1¾ pts	1 quart

Weight Conversions

25g = 1 oz
50g = 2 oz
100g = 4 oz
140g = 5 oz
175g = 6 oz
200g = 7 oz
250g = 9 oz
300g = 10 oz
400g = 14 oz
450g = 1lb
700g = 1lb 9 oz
800g = 1lb 12 oz
1kg = 2lb 4 oz

Oven Temperature Conversions

225 F = 95 C = Gas ¼
250 F = 120 C = Gas ½
275 F = 140 C – Gas 1
300 F = 150 C = Gas 2
325 F = 160 C – Gas 3
350 F = 180 C = Gas 4
375 F = 190 C – Gas 5
400 F = 200 C = Gas 6
425 F = 220 C = Gas 7
450 F = 230 C = Gas 8
475 F = 240 C = Gas 9

Ovens vary so cooking times are only approximate. Always preheat your oven and for fan-assisted ovens reduce the temperature by 20°F or see the manufacturer's instructions for your oven.

Portion Sizes

Portion sizes are a general guide but are based on the calories given. Appetites are different but if you want to lose weight you must stick to the portion size.

Oil - Water Spray

Frying in oil or fats, even shallow frying is not recommended as it can add a lot of calories to any meal. You can make up a solution of 1 part oil to 8 parts water and store it in one of those plastic bottles used as plant de-misters that you can get from any store or garden centre.

When you need to grill / broil or dry fry, a few sprays of this solution is enough to lubricate the grill / broiler wire or pan to stop the food sticking. Give the bottle a good shake before using and I recommend sunflower or rapeseed oil. You can even spray the food with this mixture to stop it drying out when you grill / broil or oven frying.

Calorie Controlled Cooking Spray

These can be widely purchased now and are really useful when you just want to coat a pan to stop food sticking, without swamping the food with oil or fat.

Gluten-free Ingredients

There are many gluten-free products in almost all of the big supermarkets now. In the UK Waitrose, Tesco and Sainsbury's carry a huge range as do the US supermarkets so you should be able to find everything listed in this cookbook quite easily.

BREAKFASTS

Personally I found it a lot easier not to eat breakfast but this is a matter of choice or your metabolism or your willpower. My partner has to eat breakfast or he feels weak and woozy. He has the porridge made with 50% milk/water with either half a banana or some stewed plums, apple or rhubarb and finds that this is enough to keep him going until lunchtime.

Just a note on Porridge oats. Unless you are celiac there really is no need to buy gluten free porridge oats as oats do not contain gluten. The reason they still carry a warning is more about contamination in the factory rather than the risk of gluten being present. Personally if you are gluten intolerant but not celiac I would buy the plain oats as they are a quarter of the price. But at the end of the day it is your choice.

If you decide to have breakfast you could elect to miss lunch so that you can have something more substantial in the morning.

Try some of the following.

A typical fasting-day breakfast of 300 calories could be two scrambled eggs with a slice of ham, a good source of protein. But this would only leave you 200 or 300 calories for the rest of the day. Try leaving out the ham and then you would only use 160 calories

Or

Gluten-free Porridge or Millet Flakes with Soy milk, raisins and honey = 224 calories, plenty of water, green tea or black coffee.

Or

1 medium banana, 170g of 0% fat Greek yogurt, 1 tsp of chopped walnuts topped with a tsp of runny honey which is only 150 calories.

Or

2 eggs, dash of soy milk, 1 tomato, 2 spring onions (scallions). Make yourself an omelette by frying the tomato and spring onions (scallions) in a spray of oil or oil and water mix, add the eggs and mix in and just cook until ready. - 180 calories

Some More Simple Breakfasts

Kippers

Serves 1 = 125 calories a portion
Preparation – 2 minutes
Cooking – 2-3 minutes

There are roughly 125 calories in an average sized smoked kipper fillet, so this will make a quick and satisfying breakfast.

Either cook as normal under the grill or for a no smell method, place in a suitable dish with a wedge of lemon, add a tbsp milk, cover with cling wrap and microwave for two and a half minutes and voila, tasty breakfast that hasn't used up too much of your allowance.

Porridge with Various

Serves 1 - 136 calories a portion
Preparation - 2 minutes
Cooking - 3 minutes

- 30g/ 1¼ oz Gluten-free porridge oats or millet flakes
- 200ml / 7 fl oz / 1 scant cup - soy milk and water mixed 50/50
- 50 gm/ 2oz grapes or 2 tbsp of stewed plums or rhubarb or half a banana
- A dribble of honey if needed but try to do without.

Method

In a large 3.5 pint jug or bowl, mix porridge oats with the water and microwave on high for 2 minutes, stir and microwave for a further minute, serve topped with one of the above fruits and the honey.

Scrambled Eggs with Various Fillings

Serves 1 = 170 calories a portion
Preparation - 2 minutes
Cooking - 3 minutes

- 2 medium eggs
- 1 medium tomato
- 1 tsp of fresh herbs to taste
- pinch of chilli flakes (optional)

Method

Chop the tomato and microwave with the chilli flakes (optional) for about 45 seconds to heat. Do your scrambled eggs how you like them but preferably not overcooked and just add the heated tomato at the end to serve.

You can also replace the tomato with either 100g mushrooms or 100g spring onions (scallions). Just slice and fry off in a small non stick pan, with just a spray of oil and add to the scrambled egg.

This may not be satisfying for everyone, but if you really need to eat something rather than go without breakfast, then this makes a change from porridge.

Fruit Platter

Serves 1 - 100-120 calories a portion

Choose 250g / 9oz of your favourite fruit such as Pink or White Grapefruit, Pineapple, Raspberries, Peaches or Nectarines, Kiwi Fruit. No Banana though.
Method
Prepare and mix together your chosen fruits and then just weigh out 250 grams for breakfast on your fasting days. You can snack on the surplus on your other days if you like or save for your second day, will keep in fridge just fine

Fruit Fool

This breakfast recipe can be adapted to seasonal fruits that are easily available in the shops. Choose from any of the following but only use 50g of each.

Serves 1 - 45- 55 calories per serving
Preparation - 2 minutes

Choose 50g / 2oz of **ONE** of the following:
blackberries - fresh peach sliced - raspberries - tinned rhubarb - strawberries
50g / 2oz 0% fat Greek yogurt
Method
Mash or chop the chosen fruit and fold into the Greek yogurt.

Egg White Omelette

Serves 1 - 57 calories per serving
Preparation - 2 minutes
Cooking - 2 minutes

- 3 large eggs
- a few basil or other fresh herb leaves chopped
- 3 sprays light sunflower oil

Method

Separate the eggs and save the yolks to use in an omelette for a non fasting day meal.

Whisk together the egg whites and a good helping of salt and pepper. Spray the oil into a non stick pan and heat until the pan looks hot. Pour in the egg whites and cook until ready but not too dry. Add the chopped herb leaves, fold over and serve at once

Low Calorie Fried Breakfast

This is a bit of a cheats fry up but when you really fancy something a bit tastier on one of your fasting days then this will hit the spot. Most supermarkets have the medallion type bacon usually classed as reduced fat. If not, just cut off the tail of the bacon and all of the fat before you cook it..

Serves 1 - 178 calories per serving
Cooking- 10 minutes

- 2 reduced fat bacon rashers
- 1 large egg
- 1 medium tomato halved

Method

Heat a non stick frying pan until hot. Add the bacon and when it starts to release some fat or liquid, swish it around the pan to coat and then add the two tomato halves. Fry for about 2 minutes or until they are both starting to brown.

Turn the bacon and tomatoes over and move to one side of the pan. Crack the egg into the space and fry for another three minutes. If the egg is not fully cooked, pop a lid or splash guard on top to help it along and then just serve.

Another Fry Up

This includes baked beans which are naturally gluten free and will bulk it up a little more.

Serves 1 - 194 calories per serving
Cooking - 5 minutes

- 1 reduced fat bacon rasher
- 1 large egg
- 100g / 4oz reduced sugar and salt baked beans

Method

Heat a small non stick frying pan on a medium heat and when hot, add the bacon to the pan. Fry for about 1 minute before turning over and then adding the egg.

Fry until the egg is cooked to your liking. In the meantime heat the baked beans in a small saucepan or better still microwave covered for 1 minute. Serve with the egg and bacon and enjoy.

EASY LUNCHES

Bacon Lettuce & Tomato Sandwich

This is a quick but satisfying lunch and you can have because it uses low fat bacon. Be careful with other brand wraps as they are quite high in calories.

173 calories per serving
Preparation - 2 minutes
Cooking - 5 minutes

- 1 gluten-free wrap
- 1 low fat bacon rasher
- 1 tsp gluten-free light mayonnaise
- 1 medium tomato
- few lettuce leaves (any type)

Method
Grill or dry fry the bacon and drain off any liquid or fat. Build the sandwich by spreading the salad cream over the wrap, top with the sliced lettuce and then bacon rasher and finally add the sliced tomato. Fold up and enjoy.

Cottage Cheese on Various

Serves 1 – 109 calories a portion plus

Choose from the following gluten-free biscuits
- Kallo Organic Rice Cakes – 30 kcal per cake
- Lovemoor Crackerbreads – 27 kcal per biscuit
- Ogran Essential Fibre Crispbread – 35 kcal per biscuit
- Any other favourite gluten-free crispbreads that have a low calorie count

- 100g Reduced Fat Cottage Cheese

Method

Calculate how many you can eat within you daily allowance. Just put your cottage cheese on and top with a sliver of cucumber or tomato, salt and pepper.

Poached Eggs with Spinach

Serves 1 – 200 calories
Preparation - 5 minutes
Cooking - 10 minutes

- 1 bag fresh spinach
- 2 eggs
- A little olive oil

Method

Poach the eggs as you like them. I find those silicone poaching pods are great and always deliver a perfect egg. Rinse the spinach in a colander or sieve and pour a kettle of boiling water over it to wilt. Drain off excess water by pressing into the colander or sieve with a potato masher or other flat tool. Place on warmed plate and top with poached eggs and season to taste.

You can use frozen spinach if more convenient, just defrost 200g naturally or if in a hurry you can microwave it, squeeze excess water out and heat gently until warmed through.

Potato Salad

Makes 1 portion - 120 calories
Preparation - 10 minutes
Cooking – 20 minutes

- 125g / 4½ oz small or new potatoes
- 1 tbsp gluten-free low-fat mayonnaise
- 1 tbsp low-fat Greek yoghurt
- ½ tsp gluten-free Dijon mustard
- 6 spring onions (scallions)
- ¼ of a cucumber

Method

Cut the potatoes into roughly 2cm chunks and bring to the boil in a pan of lightly salted water and cook for 10-15 minutes or until soft.

Mix together the mayonnaise and yogurt add the mustard and mix it in well.

Drain the potatoes and put them in a large bowl. When they have cooled a little, stir in the mayonnaise mixture and leave to cool completely.

Chop the spring onions (scallions) and cucumber and add them to the cold potato salad, mix well, season to taste and serve.

This potato salad can be made in bigger batches and served at lunch or dinner with your other chosen foods. At 120 calories a serving it makes a nice lunch with half a tin of tuna in water, drained (70cals) and a chopped tomato (10cals)

LESS THAN 200 CALORIES

The following recipes are all 200 calories or less, some are even less than 100 calories. They are substantial enough for lunch or a light evening meal and are very easy to prepare and cook.

There are also a few that you can change around a bit for a bit more variety and taste.

VEGETARIAN

Butternut Squash Soup – 150 kcal

This is a thick and warming soup that can be stored or frozen for another fasting day.

Serves 4 - 150 calories a portion
***Suitable for freezing
Preparation - 10-15 minutes
Cooking - 25-30 minutes

- 1 tsp olive oil
- 1 small onion, chopped
- 1 clove of garlic, chopped
- 1 small butternut squash – about 250g / 9oz

- 1 litre / 1¾ pints / 4 cups gluten-free vegetable stock
- 1 pinch cayenne pepper

Method

Heat the oil in a large pan. Add the onion and garlic and cook very gently for about 5 minutes until translucent and sticky but not burnt.

Prepare the squash by cutting into quarters; take out the seeds and then peel. Cut the remaining flesh into small chunks and when onion is ready, add the squash to the pan.

Stir, add the stock and cayenne pepper and bring to a low simmer. Lower the heat and cook for about 20 minutes. When squash is ready, leave to cool slightly and either use a blender or mash it by hand. Season to taste and add a little more hot stock or water if the soup is too thick.

Cauliflower Crumb Bake - 120 kcal

This is a very simple and economical dish to make and is also very low in calories.

Serves 4 – 120 calories per serving
***Suitable for freezing
Preparation - 25 minutes
Cooking - 10 minutes

- 2 courgettes
- 3 garlic cloves
- 1 tsp dried basil leaves
- 1 medium cauliflower
- 60g / 2 oz fresh gluten-free breadcrumbs
- 60g / 2oz half fat grated cheese

Method

Preheat oven to 220° C / 450°F / Gas 7

Quarter the courgettes lengthways and slice into chunky pieces. Crush the garlic and break the cauliflower into large florets. Fry the courgettes in a large pan that has been oil sprayed and heated up for 3 minutes until slightly browned. Add 1 tsp of dried herbs and 2 of the garlic cloves and cook for a further minute.

Add the tomatoes and 100 ml / 3½ fl oz boiling water and then the cauliflower florets. Season to taste and bring back to the boil, cover and simmer for 10 minutes until cauliflower is cooked.

Mix together the breadcrumbs, cheese, remaining herbs and garlic. Put the cauliflower mixture into an oven-proof dish and scatter the breadcrumb mixture on top. Spray with low calorie spray oil and bake for 10 minutes until top is golden.

*If freezing portions just put cauliflower mixture into suitable containers and the breadcrumb mixture into separate dishes. Defrost thoroughly and follow final step above.

Easy Mixed Salad - 40 kcal

You can have this salad with any of your chosen meats or fish for lunch or dinner. I also have this with an omelette either hot or cold on my non-fasting days because it is easy to make, delicious to eat and keeps me off the bread and cakes.

Serves 1 - 40 calories
Preparation 5-10 minutes

- 1 tomato
- 2 sticks celery
- 6 thick slices of cucumber,
- 2 spring onions (scallions)
- 1 tbsp of gluten-free light mayonnaise

Method

If you like, peel the celery and then chop or slice all salad ingredients. Stir mayonnaise into the prepared salad. Drizzle over a little balsamic vinegar for a bit more flavour.

Hearty Potato & Leek Soup – 150 kcal

This soup is so delicious, you really should make bigger batches of it and freeze for convenience.

Serves 1 - 150 calories a portion
***Suitable for freezing
Preparation - 15 minutes
Cooking - 45 minutes

- 250g/8oz small leeks, untrimmed
- 100g / 3½ oz potatoes
- 2 tsp olive oil
- 100g / 3½ oz button mushrooms
- A few sprigs of tarragon, stalks removed
- 80ml / 3 fl oz / ⅓ cup of soy milk

Method

Trim the leeks, cut into thin slices and place in cold water to get rid of any soil.

Peel and cut the potatoes into 2cm cubes. Heat the oil in a large pan over a medium heat.

Thoroughly drain the leeks and add to the pan. Cook gently for about 5 minutes. Add the potatoes and tarragon leaves and enough water to cover. Cook the vegetables for 15-20 minutes with the lid on, then add the milk and the sliced mushrooms and cook for another 20 minutes, adding more water if necessary.

Take out about ¼ of the soup including some potatoes and mash or whiz smooth. Return to the pan, season to taste and serve hot.

Hungarian Vegetables - 115 kcal

This is a very low calorie dish that can be kept in the fridge and eaten for quick lunches on fasting or non fasting days.

Serves 4 – 115 calories per serving
Preparation - 10 minutes
Cooking - 20 minutes

- 1 onion
- 2 garlic cloves
- 1 red & 1 green peppers
- 3 Portobello mushrooms
- 400g / 14 oz tin artichoke hearts in water
- 400g / 14 oz tin chopped tomatoes
- 1 tbsp Belazu gluten-free rose harissa paste
- 1 tbsp paprika
- 1 tbsp gluten-free tomato puree

- 300ml / 10 fl oz gluten-free vegetable stock

Method

Roughly chop the onion and crush the garlic. De-seed the peppers and cut into 8 pieces. Quarter the mushrooms, drain and quarter the artichoke hearts.

Spray a large non stick pan and heat until hot. Add the onion and cook for 4 minutes until soft but not burnt. Add the peppers, mushrooms, garlic and artichokes and cook for a further 3 minutes until browned.

Stir in the harissa paste and tomato puree with the paprika and cook for a further minute. Add the tin of tomatoes and the vegetable stock, bring to a simmer and cook for 10 minutes until thickened.

Serve at once.

Italian Aubergines - 135 kcal

This is a very low calorie but really filling lunch dish. You could also use is as a vegetable dish with some alternative main dish. It can even be left to go cold overnight in the fridge and eaten with a salad.

Serves 4 – 135 calories per serving
***Suitable for freezing
Preparation - 20 minutes plus cooling
Cooking - 40 minutes

- 1 medium onion
- 500g / 1lb 2oz aubergines / eggplant
- 1 tsp dried mixed herbs
- 400g / 14 oz tin chopped tomatoes
- 1 tbsp syrup
- 50g / 1¾ oz pitted green or black olives
- 1 tbsp red wine vinegar

Method

Slice the onion finely, dice the aubergines, rinse and chop the olives.

Spray a frying pan with the cooking spray and fry the onion for roughly 3-4 minutes until soft. Add the chopped aubergine and dried mixed herbs and cook for another 5-6 minutes, turning often.

Add the rest of the ingredients, bring to the boil and cover and simmer for 35 minutes. Add salt and pepper to taste.

Lentil & Spring Greens Soup – 110 kcal

The lentils and greens make a colourful combination and the taste is not bad either. Alternate the choice of greens and spinach for variety.

Serves 2 - 110 calories
Preparation - 10 minutes
Cooking 30-35 minutes

- 100g / 3¼ oz green lentils
- 1 medium onion
- 2 cloves of garlic
- 1 tsp olive oil
- 100g / 3¼ oz fresh spring greens or spinach
- 400ml / 13oz / 1¾ cups gluten-free vegetable stock

Method

Rinse the lentils under running water and cook them in fresh water for 10-15 minutes until just beginning to go soft. Drain and rinse again.

Peel and chop the onion and garlic. Put the oil in a large pan and cook the onion until soft but not burnt, then add the garlic and lentils.

Wash and chop the greens or spinach and add it to the pan gradually, allowing it to shrink down but keep stirring. When all the greens or spinach are in, reduce it by about half, add enough liquid to cover and cook for about 15 minutes if spring greens, 10 minutes if using spinach.

Allow to cool slightly, blend, reheat and serve.

Low Calorie Hummus – 125 kcal

Hummus is a great little snacking or lunch food. It is quite filling if you have 3 rice cakes at 30 calories each with a thin slice of cucumber or tomato on top.

Makes 4 portions - 125 calories per portion
Preparation 5-10 minutes
Cooking 5 minutes

- 1 x 400g/14oz tin gluten-free chickpeas
- 2 cloves of garlic
- juice of 1 lemon
- 2 tbsp gluten-free tahini

Method
Drain and rinse the chickpeas. Put them in a pan with fresh water and heat gently for about 5 minutes.

Drain the chickpeas but keep some of the liquid and set aside.

Crush the garlic, place in a food processor with the chickpeas and lemon juice. Add the tahini and a tablespoon of the cooking liquid and process until smooth, adding more liquid if necessary.

For dipping per person:

½ red pepper, de-seeded and sliced into batons

2 inches cucumber, cut into batons

½ carrot, peeled and cut into batons

Mini Cheese Soufflé - 150 kcal

You can have these delicious cheese pots as a starter or better still for lunch with a green salad or steamed spinach.

Serves 2 – 150 calories per serving
Preparation - 15 minutes
Cooking - 15 minutes

- 40g / 1½ oz fresh gluten-free breadcrumbs
- 1 egg
- 1 tsp gluten-free wholegrain mustard
- 100ml / 3½ oz skimmed milk
- 40g / 1½ oz low fat cheddar cheese

Method

Preheat oven to 190°C / 375° F / Gas Mark 5

Beat the eggs and grate the cheese.

Mix all the ingredients together, season with salt and freshly ground pepper and divide between 2 ramekin dishes. Leave to stand for 5 minutes.

When oven is ready, bake for 15 minutes until the soufflés have risen slightly. Serve at once with the salad or steamed broccoli.

Mixed Salad with Avocado – 120 kcal

A simple salad that goes with anything. Try it on its own for lunch or with a salmon or Tuna steak for your evening meal.

Serves 1 - 120 calories
Preparation - 5 minutes

- 60- 80gm bag mixed salad leaves or rocket
- 3 small tomatoes
- 1 small or half a medium ripe avocado
- Selection of fresh herbs such as basil, mint or chives (optional)
- Olive oil and balsamic vinegar for drizzling

Method

Slice or quarter the tomatoes, wash and shred the mixed salad. Mix with the herbs if using and place in a good sized bowl. Peel and slice the avocado, lay on top of the salad and drizzle with the dressing.

Moroccan Spicy Tofu - 195 calories

Serves 4 – 195 calories per serving
***Suitable for freezing
Preparation - 5 minutes
Cooking - 20 minutes

- 1tsp oil
- 1 red onion
- ½ tsp ground cinnamon
- 1 tsp ground cumin
- 300g / 10oz Clearspring organic gluten-free tofu or other firm tofu
- 1 tbsp gluten-free flour
- 450ml / 16 fl oz gluten-free vegetable stock
- zest and juice of ½ lemon
- 410g / 14oz tin Mr Organic or other gluten-free chickpeas

- bunch flat leaf parsley

Method

Chop the onion and drain and rinse the chickpeas. Cube or slice the tofu.

Heat a large pan and fry the onion in the oil for about 4-5 minutes until soft but not burnt.

Add the flour, spices and cook for a further 1 minute. Add the stock, lemon zest and juice and the chickpeas and bring to the boil.

Add the tofu and cook for 5 minutes stirring occasionally. If too thick, add a little hot water. When ready, add the roughly chopped parsley and serve hot.

Pea and Spinach Dahl – 160 kcal

This dish will warm and fill you up on your fasting day, what more could you want?

Serves 4- 160 calories per serving
***Suitable for freezing
Preparation - 10 minutes
Cooking - 50 minutes

- 1 large onion
- 4 cloves garlic
- 1 thumb size piece fresh ginger
- 1 large red chilli
- 1 tbsp sunflower oil
- 225g / 8oz red lentils
- ¼ tsp turmeric powder
- ¼ tsp cayenne pepper

- 1 tsp paprika
- ½ tsp ground cumin
- 1200ml / 2 pints water
- 1 tomato
- juice of 1 lime
- 2 tbsp frozen peas
- 3 cubes frozen spinach

Method

Peel and roughly chop the onion, garlic and ginger. Do the same to the chilli but if you don't want it too hot you can remove all or some of the seeds and membrane.

Heat the oil in a heavy based pan and sauté all chopped ingredients for about 5 minutes or until the onion has softened. Add all the ground spices and fry for another couple of minutes stirring well.

Rinse the lentils in a sieve under cold running water for at least a minute and add them to the pan. Stir really well and then add the water and bring back to a boil. Boil at a steady rate for 10 minutes and then turn the heat down to a low simmer.

Continue to simmer at the lowest heat for about 30 to 40 minutes, making sure you stir the Dahl often to stop it sticking on the bottom of the pan. The mixture will thicken as it cooks and when it looks like thick rice pudding, add the spinach, peas, lime juice and the chopped tomato and cook for another 5 minutes and then serve in warmed bowls.

Ratatouille – 105 kcal

This dish can be served with any fish or meat for a substantial evening meal as the ratatouille is only 105 calories per serving. You can have a lean pork steak or grilled chicken breast or salmon fillet or any other meat or fish choice. You could even have a medium jacket potato which is 136 calories per 100g. Just check the weight when choosing. You could add it to a couple of eggs and make a tasty crepe for lunch or supper. On a non-fasting day it is delicious on a bed of gluten-free pasta.

Serves 2 – 105 calories per portion for the ratatouille
Preparation - 10-15 minutes
Cooking - 20 minutes plus time to cook chosen meat/fish if having.

- 1 medium onion
- 1 garlic clove
- 1 small green bell pepper
- 1 small yellow bell pepper
- 1 medium courgette
- 100g / 4oz button mushrooms
- 400g / 14oz can chopped tomatoes
- 2 tbsp gluten-free tomato puree
- 1 tsp of dried mixed herbs

Method

Peel and chop the onion, trim, deseed and dice both peppers and the courgette. Half the mushrooms, chop the garlic.

Put all vegetables into a pan and add the chopped tomatoes and tomato paste and stir well. Add the dried herbs, a tsp of sugar and plenty of seasoning. Bring to the boil and simmer uncovered for 20 minutes.

Spicy Veggie Burgers - 170 kcal

These vegetable burgers are super easy to make and are delicious served with a green salad of your choice and a chopped tomato with low calorie dressing.

Serves 2 – 170 calories per serving
Preparation - 10 minutes
Cooking - 40 minutes

- 200g / 7oz butternut squash
- 200g / 7 oz potatoes
- 1 egg
- ½ tsp ground cumin
- ½ tsp chilli powder
- 1 tbsp chopped flat leaf parsley
- 2 spring onions (scallions)

Method

Peel, de-seed and dice the butternut squash, peel and dice the potatoes and finely slice the spring onions (scallions).

Bring a large pan of water to the boil and add the squash and potatoes. Bring back to a boil, cover and simmer for 10 minutes or until both are tender. At the same time boil the egg in a small saucepan of boiling water for the same time, remove from the heat and run under cold water.

Drain the squash and potatoes, rinse in cold water to stop them overcooking and drain again when cold. Return to the pan and mash or put through a potato ricer until smooth.

Peel the egg and roughly chop, then add to the squash mixture together with the spices, onions and parsley. Season well to taste and shape into 4 small burgers. Heat a non stick pan, spray with a low calorie cooking spray and cook gently for 4-5 minutes until golden brown making sure you turn a couple of times to avoid burning.

Serve with a green salad, 1 chopped tomato and a sprinkling of chilli flakes if liked.

Thai Split Pea & Carrot Soup - 125 kcal

This soup can be done in big batches as it's ideal for freezing and putting into individual portions.

Serves 4 – 125 calories per serving
***Suitable for freezing
Preparation - 35 minutes plus overnight soaking
Cooking – 1 - 1¼ hours

- 50g / 2oz yellow split peas
- 15ml / 1tbsp any light oil
- 1 small onion
- 1 garlic clove
- thumb size piece fresh ginger
- 1 red chilli
- 1½ tsp gluten-free Thai curry paste
- 225g / 8oz carrots

- 1 medium potato
- chopped coriander to serve

Method

Soak the split peas overnight in twice their volume of cold water. Peel and chop the onion, potato, carrots and garlic. De-seed and chop the red chilli and grate the fresh ginger.

Drain the split peas and thoroughly rinse. Place in a large saucepan with 1.5 litres (2½ pints) of cold water and bring to the boil. Boil rapidly for 10 minutes then reduce the heat to a gentle simmer for a further 30 minutes.

Tomato & Courgette Bake - 185 kcal

A tasty and very low calorie dish to use as a main course or as an accompaniment for a veggie main dish. You can use ready made pesto sauce or the freshly made sauce in this cookbook.

Serves 4 - 185 calories a portion
Preparation - 10-15 minutes
Cooking - 30 - 35minutes

- 500g courgettes or zucchini
- 1 clove of garlic
- 400g tomatoes
- 2 tbsp gluten-free green basil pesto
- 4 tbsp fresh gluten-free breadcrumbs
- 25g mature cheddar

Method

Pre-heat the oven to 220° or Gas 7

Top and tail then thinly slice the courgettes. Slice the tomatoes and grate the cheese.

Mix the courgette slices and pesto sauce until lightly coated. Arrange the courgette and tomato slices in a single layer in a 2 litre oven proof dish and season well.

In a separate bowl mix together the breadcrumbs, finely chopped garlic and cayenne pepper and cover the vegetables with this mixture. Drizzle with a little olive oil.

Bake for 30 minutes until golden on top and the vegetables are cooked.

Tomato and Red Pepper Soup – 95 kcal

This makes a great starter or a light lunch and is very easy to make.

Serves 4 - 95 calories per serving
***Suitable for freezing
Preparation - 10 minutes
Cooking - 30 minutes

- 2 red peppers
- 2 garlic cloves
- 1 medium onion
- 1 tsp olive oil
- 400g / 14oz tin of chopped tomatoes
- 75g / 3oz potatoes

Method

De-seed and chop the peppers into chunks. Chop or dice the onion and the garlic. Peel and cut the potatoes into good sized chunks and keep in water until needed.

Heat a pan over a medium heat and when warm, add the peppers, onion and garlic and allow them to cook for about 5 minutes until softened.

Make sure you stir often so that they don't stick. Add the tinned tomatoes and potatoes and using the tomato can as a measure use 2 cans full of water to cover.

Simmer the soup for about 20 minutes until the vegetables are done, then allow them to cool slightly and blend until smooth. Reheat and serve.

This makes 4 portions but can be frozen for another fasting day

Tzatsiki – 50 kcal

A versatile and quick to prepare dip or salsa that will go with most fish and meat dishes or any salads.

Serves 2 - 50 calories per portion
Preparation - 10 minutes

- half medium cucumber
- 1 cloves of garlic
- a handful of flat-leaved parsley or coriander
- a few mint leaves
- 100ml / 3oz / ⅓ cup low-fat Greek yogurt
- 1/2 tsp olive oil
- cayenne and black pepper

Method

Cut the cucumber in half across, and then cut each part in half lengthwise. Remove the seeds and chop the cucumber finely.

Chop the herbs and garlic and put them in a bowl, then add the cucumber. Stir everything together really well.

Add the yogurt and again mix well. Drizzle the olive oil on top and sprinkle with half tsp cayenne and some freshly ground black pepper.

Vegetable and Citrus Soup - 80 kcal

This tasty soup is a real tummy filler for lunch or an afternoon snack. I suggest you make this in bulk and freeze in individual portions so that you always have a ready prepared meal to hand.

Makes 6 portions – 80 calories per serving
***Suitable for freezing
Preparation - 20 minutes
Cooking - 25 minutes

- 500g / 1lb 2oz carrots
- 1 swede
- 2 onions
- 2 garlic cloves
- juice and zest of 1 orange

- 1½ litres / 2¾ pints gluten-free vegetable stock
- 1 tbsp red wine vinegar
- 1 tbsp gluten-free tomato puree
- bunch chives, chopped

Method

Peel and dice the carrots and swede. Chop the onions and crush the garlic.

Put the vegetables, garlic, tomato puree and vinegar into a large pan, pour over the hot vegetable stock and stir thoroughly. Bring back to a simmer and cook on a low heat for 15- 20 minutes or until vegetables are cooked.

Stir in the orange juice and zest together with the chopped chives and serve in warm bowls for a delicious and filling lunch or afternoon snack.

Vegetable Curry – 180 kcal

This should be made in bigger portions and frozen. You could also use fresh vegetables; adjust the cooking time to make sure they are cooked before serving the curry.

Serves 1 - 180 calories per serving
***Suitable for freezing
Preparation 5 minutes
Cooking 40 minutes

- 1 tsp sunflower oil
- ½ tsp each of cumin seeds and mustard seeds
- ½ onion
- 1 clove garlic
- ¼ tsp ground coriander, ground cumin and turmeric

- ½ tsp mild chilli powder
- ½ tsp salt
- ½ tin chopped tomatoes
- 2 handfuls of pre-chopped frozen vegetables (choose from carrot, peas, green beans, cauliflower, or anything else you like!)

Method

Finely chop the onion and garlic. Heat the oil and cook the cumin and mustard seeds until the spices start to pop but do not burn them.

Add the chopped onion and garlic, stir and lower the heat to a simmer.

Cook the onions for about 10 minutes until they are translucent and starting to go brown. Add the remaining spices and the salt, stir thoroughly and then add the chopped tomatoes.

Add your choice of vegetables and then simmer gently for 30 minutes adding a little water if mixture starts to dry out.

FISH

Canned Tuna Salad – 146 kcal

When we first started the 5:2 diet we had this for lunch every fasting day. It is very tasty and filling and we still have it often because it is so simple to do. We sometimes substitute the tuna for a 2 egg omelette which we leave to go cold and chop it up.

Serves 1 - 146 calories
Preparation - 5 minutes

- 1 tomato
- 2 sticks celery
- 5 thick slices of cucumber,
- 1 spring onion
- ½ tin of tuna in spring water drained
- 1 tbsp of gluten-free light mayonnaise

Method

Chop or slice all salad ingredients to the size and shape you prefer. Mix the mayonnaise into the Tuna and stir into the prepared salad. (You can keep the other half in the fridge and use for your next fasting day lunch or use it for a sandwich on a non fasting day.)

Mussels in Tasty Sauce – 185 kcal

New Zealand cooked mussels are large but if you can't find them, use other fresh mussels instead and steam them just the same. See below for preparation of live mussels. This dish makes a delicious and low calorie starter or for a non fasting day you can add some crusty bread for a more substantial supper.

Serves 2 – 185 Calories per serving
Preparation - 10 minutes
Cooking - 30 minutes

- 1 tbsp olive oil
- 1 small onion

- 1 clove garlic
- 1 small red pepper
- Sprig of rosemary
- 2 bay leaves
- 75ml / 3oz / or ⅓ cup white wine
- 1 small courgette or zucchini
- 400g / 14oz can of chopped tomatoes
- 1 tbsp gluten-free tomato puree
- ½ tsp sugar
- 25g / 1oz pitted black olives
- 350g / 12oz New Zealand cooked mussels in their shells
- little zest of an orange

Method

Finely chop the onion. Garlic and pepper and gently fry for 4 minutes in the oil until softened. Add the rosemary and bay leaves with the tomatoes, half of the white wine and then season and bring to the boil. Add the courgette, tomato puree, sugar and olives and simmer gently for 10 minutes.

While this is simmering place the muscles in a streamer and cook over a pan of boiling water covered with a lid. Cook until the mussels all open; throw any away that do not open as they will be bad.

Remove from heat and arrange in a warmed bowl. Take out the rosemary and bay leaves and spoon sauce over the mussels.

NOTE:

If you are using live mussels, soak them in a bowl of lightly salted water for an hour. Rinse under cold running water and remove any sand by rubbing them lightly with a soft brush.

Using a sharp knife remove any 'beards' from the shells. Throw out any broken shells or any opened ones that don't close if tapped firmly with a knife handle

These are dead and must not be eaten as they can cause food poisoning. Rinse the mussels again, drain and put to one side in a colander.

Prawn and Fennel Soup – 110 kcal

This is a delicious soup that can be served hot or cold.

Serves 2 – 110 calories per serving
Preparation - 15 minutes
Cooking - 40 minutes

- 1 tsp olive oil
- 1 small onion
- 1 large fennel bulb
- 1 small potato
- 425ml / 15 fl oz or 1¾ cups water
- 200ml / 7 fl oz / or ¾ cup gluten-free passata
- 75g / 3 oz cooked small peeled prawns
- 1 medium tomato
- fresh dill

Method

Halve and slice the onion and the fennel bulb. Peel and dice the potato. Skin, de-seed and chop the tomato. Sauté the onion and fennel in the olive oil for about 4 minutes.

Add the potato, water and tomato juice, season with salt. Bring to a simmer and cook on a low heat for about 20-25 minutes, stirring occasionally until the vegetables are cooked.

Let the soup cool slightly and remove the vegetables with a slotted spoon and puree using a food blender or mash with a fork or potato masher until smooth.

Return the puree to the remaining liquid, add the prawns and heat very gently for a few minutes until the soup is heated through. Snip the dill and stir in the chopped tomato, season to taste and serve.

Tuna and White Bean Salad – 160 kcal

This makes a tasty substantial lunch or will accompany any meat or fish portion

Serves 2 - 160 calories a portion
Preparation - 10 minutes
Cooking - 5 minutes

- ½ x 400g / 14oz tin of gluten-free cannellini or other white bean
- 1-2 cloves garlic, chopped
- 1 tsp olive oil
- 3 sun-dried tomatoes in oil
- 1 small onion
- 1 x 185g / 7oz tin of tuna in spring water

- 1-2 tbsp balsamic vinegar
- Juice of one lemon

Method

Heat the olive oil and sauté the garlic for about 30 seconds. Add the drained and rinsed white beans and about half of the lemon juice and warm over a very gentle heat for about 2-3 minutes.

Meanwhile, blot the sun-dried tomatoes of excess oil using kitchen paper and cut into thin strips. Peel and finely chop the onion and add to a bowl with the tomatoes and the partly drained flaked tuna.

Remove the beans from the heat and add them to the bowl. Mix everything together and then add the balsamic vinegar and the rest of the lemon juice, stir and allow the mixture to cool before serving the salad on a large bed of your favourite lettuce leaves.

Cabbage & Prawns – 180 kcal

This dish is so quick and easy and I had almost forgotten about it as a very low calorie meal. We used to have this a lot when the cabbage was in season and had a good sized solid heart. Very economical and the prawns lift it out of the ordinary.

Serves 2 – 180 calories per serving
Preparation – 5 minutes
Cooking – 15-20 minutes

- 400g / 14oz sweetheart cabbage or other greens
- 150g fresh or cooked jumbo king prawns
- 1 medium onion
- 1 tsp oil
- splash of balsamic vinegar

Method

Remove the outer leaves of the cabbage and cut in half lengthways. Remove the hard core from the centre of the cabbage and then slice it thinly from the tip to the stalk end, discarding any chunky stalk bits. . Wash the cabbage in a bowl of cold water and drain.

Halve and slice the onion and in a wok or large deep sided frying pan heat the oil and fry the onion for about 3 minutes on a medium heat until starting to soften.

Add the cabbage and stir well to bring the onions from the base of the pan. Add the balsamic vinegar, plenty of salt and pepper and then cover the pan and continue to cook for about 5 minutes stirring occasionally.

Check the cabbage is not burning, there should be enough liquid from the cabbage by this time. Carry on cooking on a medium heat, until the cabbage stalks are softened.

When cabbage is cooked to your liking, add the prawns. If using raw prawns, continue cooking the dish until they have turned pink and are cooked inside. If using cooked prawns, only heat them through for a couple of minutes at most. Serve on warmed plates with another dash of balsamic on top.

MEAT & POULTRY

Chicken Tarragon & Lemon – 175 kcal

Chicken cooked in tarragon and lemon is a match made in heaven. Just have a crisp green salad in place of the steamed vegetables if preferred.

Serves 1 - 175 calories
Preparation - 10 minutes
Cooking - 30 minutes

- Juice and zest of ½ lemon
- Small handful of tarragon, stalks removed.
- 2 tsp olive oil
- 125g / 4½ oz skinless chicken breast

- 60ml / 2 fl oz / ¼ cup of gluten-free chicken stock

Method

Preheat the oven to 200°C/gas mark 6. Mix the lemon juice, tarragon leaves and olive oil together in a bowl and roll the chicken breast in it.

Put in a small oven-proof dish, add the stock around the base of the chicken breast, being careful not to wash off the coating mixture. Pour over any remaining lemon juice and tarragon mixture.

Cover the dish with foil and bake the chicken for 15 minutes. Remove the foil and cook for another 15 minutes, or until the chicken is done.

Slice the chicken and serve with a generous helping of steamed broccoli and courgettes as they have very few calories or a crisp green salad.

Curry Coated Chicken – 176 kcal

A dish that can be eaten hot or cold. Serve with a ratatouille or steamed vegetables or cold with a green salad and the relish

Serves 2 – 176 calories per serving
Preparation - 15 minutes
Cooking - 30-35 minutes

- 2 chicken breasts, boneless and skinless
- 1 garlic clove
- 1.25cm or ½ inch piece of fresh ginger
- ½ green chilli
- 3 tbsp low-fat natural yoghurt
- ½ tsp ground turmeric

- ½ tsp garam masala
- 2 tsp lime juice
- 2 tsp gluten-free tomato puree
- wedges of lime or lemon

Relish

- 2 medium tomatoes
- ¼ of small cucumber
- ½ small red onion
- 1 tbsp chopped flat leafed parsley (optional)

Method

Preheat the oven to 190c / 375F / Gas 5

Crush the garlic clove, peel and finely chop the fresh ginger, deseed and finely chop the green chilli. Mix them together in a bowl with the yogurt, tomato paste, spices, lime juice and seasoning.

Place the chicken breasts on a baking tray and brush them with the paste until covered all over. Bake for 30-35 minutes until the chicken is cooked through.

Make the relish as the chicken is cooking. Finely chop the tomatoes, onion and cucumber and combine with the parsley. Season and chill until needed.

When the chicken is cooked, remove and drain on kitchen paper and serve hot with the relish and lime wedges. Or you can allow to cool and serve with a green salad.

Cover the tin with a layer of very lightly greased kitchen foil and put into a deep sided roasting tin. Pour enough boiling water in the roasting tin to come halfway up the loaf tin sides.

Bake in the oven for 1-1½ hours but remove the foil lid for the last 20 minutes. Check if cooked by inserting a skewer into the loaf and of ready the juices will be clear. The loaf should also shrink slightly if ready.

Leave to cook slightly and then turn out onto a warmed plate and serve.

Pork and Apple Medallions -192 kcal

Apple and Pork go together well as the apple aids the digestion. Choose a sweet eating apple to complement the pork fillet.

Serves 2 – 192 calories per serving
Preparation – 5 minutes
Cooking – 30-40 minutes

- 4 x 50g / 1¾ oz pork medallions
- 1 tsp oil
- 1 small onion
- ½ tsp sugar
- ½ tsp dried sage
- 150ml / 5 fl oz / ⅔ cup gluten-free chicken stock
- 1 red skin apple

- ½ tsp lemon juice

Method

Halve and finely slice the onion.

Fry the onion in the oil in a frying pan for about 5 minutes then add the sugar and cook for another 3-4 minutes until golden.

Add the pork and fry 2 minutes each side until browned. Add the sage and stock, bring to a simmer and cook for 20 minutes.

While the pork is cooking, core the apple and cut into quarters and then in half again so you have 8 pieces. Add to the pan and mix in, then cook for another 4-5 minutes until the apples are tender.

Serve with fresh streamed broccoli or a green salad.

Pork with Pine Nuts – 200 kcal

Another quick and simple but impressive dish to cook for the family or for friends and it just creeps into the 200 calorie range.

Serves 4 – 200 calories per serving
Preparation – 5 minutes
Cooking – 15 minutes

- 500g / 1lb.2oz lean pork fillet
- Small bunch flat leaf parsley
- 2 tbsp olive oil
- 25g / 1oz pine nuts
- 1 lemon
- 1 tbsp clear honey

Method

Cut the pork fillet into 2cm / ¾ inch thick slices and lightly coat with the seasoned flour, shaking off any excess.

Heat half the oil in a large frying pan and cook the pork for 3 minutes each side in a single layer until nicely browned. Remove from the pan and keep warm.

Put the remaining oil into the pan and fry the pine nuts until lightly done. Stir in all of the juice of the lemon and the zest of half of it and stir in the honey as well. Combine to make a sauce.

Return the pork to the pan and scatter with the chopped parsley and cook for a further 3 minutes. Turn the pork during this time so that it is heated through.

Serve with a green salad if fasting or some tagliatelle or other flat pasta to those who are not.

Turkey and Vegetable Loaf – 180 kcal

An impressive but easy to make dish, that you can serve as a light supper meal for friends. Cook some baby new potatoes for them and just have some broccoli for yourself. Alternatively, freeze the other portions for a quick and low calorie lunch.

Serves 6 – 180 calories per serving
***Suitable for freezing
Preparation – 10 minutes
Cooking - 1-1½ hours

- 1 medium onion
- 1 garlic clove
- 900g / 2lb minced turkey
- 1 tbsp chopped fresh flat leaf parsley
- 1 tbsp chopped fresh chives

- 1 tbsp chopped fresh basil
- 1 egg white
- 1 medium courgette
- 2 medium tomatoes

Method

Preheat the oven to 190°C / 375°F / Gas 5

Finely chop the onion and crush the garlic. Lightly grease a loaf tin and line it with baking parchment.

Mix the onion, garlic, herbs and turkey together in a large bowl and season with salt and freshly ground pepper. When well mixed, add the egg white to bind it together. You may want to use your hands to get it mixed well.

Divide the mixture in two and press one portion into the tin, firming it into the corners. Thinly slice the courgette and arrange over the meat. Thinly slice the tomatoes and layer on the courgette. Put the remaining turkey on top of this and press down to firm.

Cover with foil and place in a roasting tin. Pour enough boiling water into the tin to come half way up the meatloaf tin sides. Bake in the oven for 1-1¼ hours removing the foil for the final 20 minutes.

Test the meatloaf is cooked by inserting a knife or skewer into the centre of the loaf. The loaf is cooked if the juices are clear and the loaf has shrunk away from the sides of the tin.

Serve with a good portion of steamed broccoli and courgettes

Vegetable & Meat Soup – 180 kcal

This soup will be very welcome on any type of day. You can use your favourite meat but make sure it is very lean. This recipe has 4 servings but it is so delicious it won't be around long. Either keep in the fridge or can be frozen for another fasting day.

Serves 4 – 180 calories per portion
***Suitable for freezing
Preparation - 10 minutes
Cooking - 35 minutes

- 60g / 2½ oz red lentils
- 1.2 litres / 2 pints / 5 cups gluten-free beef stock

- 1 tsp dried mixed herbs
- 225g / 8oz lean rump or sirloin steak or lean lamb or pork fillet
- 1 large carrot
- 100g button mushrooms
- 1 leek
- 1 medium onion
- 2 sticks or celery
- salt & pepper
- 2 tbsp fresh flat leaf parsley – chopped

Method

Cut all of the fat from your chosen meat and cut into thin strips.

Dice the carrot, cut the leek in half length ways and wash under cold water to remove any dirt, then cut into 4" pieces and shred length ways. Chop the onion, and then slice the celery.

Add the red lentils to the stock in a large saucepan with the dried herbs, bring to a simmer and cook for 10 minutes on a low heat with the lid on.

Add the prepared vegetables and the meat to the pan and bring back to the boil, and simmer covered for 15 minutes. Add the mushrooms and cook for a further 5 minutes.

Skim any floating fat or scum from the pan as it cooks and when finished soak up floating fat with kitchen paper.

Serve in deep bowls topped with the parsley.

LESS THAN 300 CALORIES

The following recipes are less than 300 calories. These are all substantial enough for lunch or evening meal and are easy to prepare and cook.

There are a few here that you can adapt using different vegetables for a bit more variety and taste.

VEGETARIAN

Chilli Beans - 200 kcal

This is so easy to make because it uses ready cooked beans and tomatoes. Make enough to freeze for another day.

Serves 4 – 200 calories per serving
***Suitable for freezing
Preparation - 20 minutes
Cooking - 35 minutes

- 1 tbsp olive oil
- 1 medium onion
- 2 garlic cloves
- 175g / 6 oz carrots
- 1 red pepper

- 1 green pepper
- 150g / 5½ oz button mushrooms
- 1 cooking apple
- 2 tbsp chilli powder
- 225g / 7½ oz chopped tomatoes
- 400g / 14 oz can Mr Organic or other gluten-free mixed beans

Method

Halve and slice the onion, crush the garlic, peel and dice the carrot, de-seed and dice both peppers, quarter the button mushrooms and peel, core and grate the apple.

Heat the oil in a large pan and cook the onion, garlic, carrots, peppers and mushrooms for 5 minutes.

Stir in the grated apple and the chilli powder and cook for a further 2 minutes stirring well.

Add the tomatoes and mixed beans, stir well and simmer with the lid on for 30 minutes. Make sure you keep an eye on it as it will tend to stick to the pan so stir it quite often.

Five Bean Wrap – 294 kcal

This is a very filling meal and can be eaten for lunch or dinner depending on your schedule. Most food shops now stock many different types of ready cooked beans in either cans or pouches. Try a tin of the mixed bean salad variety which lends itself very well to this recipe.

Serves 1 - 294 calories per serving
Preparation 5 minutes

- 1 gluten-free wrap
- 80g / 3oz gluten-free mixed beans
- 20g / ¾ oz low calorie or lighter cheddar cheese
- 1 tbsp any gluten-free salsa
- shredded lettuce

Method

Rinse and drain the beans. Spread your chosen salsa evenly over the whole wrap.

Add the drained beans, but leave at least an 2 inch area free at the bottom of the wrap so that you can fold it over easier.

Put the lettuce on top of the beans and finally grate the cheese evenly over the lettuce. Fold up the bottom of the wrap and roll up the rest.

You may wish to warm the wrap up a bit first as it will be easier to roll but this is not essential.

Hearty Summer Salad – 294 kcal

This recipe serves 3 because you are using canned beans. It will keep in the fridge if you want to just use 1 or 2 portions or if you can get smaller tins of beans then adjust accordingly. Use medium tomatoes instead of large and half a medium onion. Everything else is fine as it is.

Serves 3 – 294 calories a portion
Preparation - 5-10 minutes

- 400g / 14 oz. can gluten-free chickpeas
- 400g / 14 oz. can gluten-free cannellini Beans
- 300g / 11 oz jar artichoke hearts
- 2 large tomatoes
- ½ large onion
- 3 large fresh garlic cloves

- olive oil and balsamic vinegar
- a few pinches of dried parsley
- 150g / 5 oz mixed salad leaves

Method

Drain chickpeas and cannellini beans and put them into a large bowl. Chop artichoke hearts (into eighths if they're whole, or into quarters if they're already halved) and add to bowl.

Chop the tomatoes, dice the onion and crush garlic gloves and add these also to the bowl.

Whip olive oil and balsamic vinegar together, and then pour over the pile in the bowl. Add a few generous pinches of dried parsley, then salt and pepper to taste.

Stir all the ingredients thoroughly with a large spoon to distribute them evenly and coat them with vinaigrette. Season to taste and serve on a bed of mixed salad.

Leek & Bean Frittata - 215 kcal

An easy dish to make and keeps well in the fridge and is just as delicious cold for a quick lunch for your next fasting day.

Serves 4 – 215 calories per serving
Preparation - 10 minutes
Cooking - 40 minutes

- 250g / 9oz fresh or frozen broad beans (defrosted)
- 2 leeks
- 2 courgettes
- 1 tbsp fresh mint leaves
- 6 eggs
- 75g / 2¾ oz light mozzarella cheese

Method

Slice the leeks and wash out any soil. Thinly slice the courgettes and chop the mint. Drain the mozzarella and cut into very small cubes.

Add the broad beans to a pan of boiling water, bring back to the boil and cook for 4 minutes, add the leeks and courgettes and cook for a further 2 minutes. Drain and run under cold water to cool. Peel the outer skin from the beans and discard.

Heat a large non-stick pan and fry the vegetables with the mint for 3 minutes to remove excess water. Beat the eggs and season with salt and freshly ground black pepper. Pour into the pan and cook gently for 5-6 minutes or until nearly set.

Meanwhile, preheat a grill to medium, sprinkle the frittata with the chopped mozzarella, brown under the grill until top is bubbling.

Slice into 8 portions and serve 2 per person with a green salad or fresh steamed broccoli.

Mushroom Omelette & Salad – 255 kcal

Serves 1 – 255 calories
Preparation - 5-10 minutes
Cooking - 5-7 minutes

- 75g / 3 oz mushrooms
- 2 medium free range eggs
- Handful of fresh Basil or other preferred herb
- 75g / 3 oz mixed leaf or other salad
- 5 cherry or other small tomatoes
- Dribble of olive oil and balsamic vinegar dressing

Method

Slice or chop the mushrooms and cook in a non stick pan until soft but not shrunk too much, remove from pan and set aside.

Wipe out pan and spray with the 1 cal spray oil that you can get from most supermarkets. Lightly beat the eggs together and when pan is hot add the eggs.

Draw the eggs from the side into the middle of the pan until most of the egg liquid has gone from the top of the omelette.

Sprinkle the mushrooms on top evenly, season with salt and freshly ground pepper and when the bottom of the omelette is slightly browned, fold in half, lower heat to minimum and leave to cook very gently for about 2 minutes.

Serve with the mixed salad, tomatoes and dressing.

Mushroom Risotto – 284 kcal

This risotto uses brown rice which is a great source of vitamin B. It is also lower in calories than white rice.

Serves 2 – 284 calories per serving
***Suitable for freezing
Preparation - 20 minutes
Cooking - 50 minutes

- 10g / ½ oz dried porcini mushrooms
- 225g / 8 oz mixed mushrooms
- 15ml or 1 tbsp olive oil
- 1 small onion
- 1 garlic clove
- 125g / 4½ oz brown long grain rice
- 450ml / 16 fl oz / 1 pint gluten-free vegetable stock
- 2 tbsp chopped fresh flat leaf parsley

Method

Put the dried porcini mushrooms in a bowl and pour over 150ml / ½ cup hot water. Soak for about 20 minutes or until the mushrooms have fully hydrated. Drain but reserve the juice and add it to the stock. Roughly chop the mushrooms.

Finely chop the onion and garlic and using a large pan, sauté in the oil for about 5 minutes on a low heat, stirring to avoid burning. Add the rice to the onion mixture and stir well to coat with the oil.

Add the stock, bring to a simmer, lower the heat and cook for 20 minutes or until the liquid has almost gone. Make sure you stir frequently to avoid the risotto sticking to the pan.

Cut the remaining mushrooms into quarters or smaller if using a mixture of larger mushrooms. Add to the rice and stir really well to mix in.

Cook for a further 10-15 minutes until all the liquid has been absorbed. Check that the rice has cooked through, adding more hot water or stock if necessary.

Season to taste and add the chopped parsley before serving.

Nutty Mushroom Pilaf - 298 kcal

Using brown rice for a delicious nutty flavour makes this dish very filling. You can also use dried porcini or other mixed mushrooms instead of the flat mushrooms.

Serves 2 – 298 calories per serving
Preparation - 5 minutes
Cooking - 30 minutes

- 4 large flat mushrooms
- 1 onion
- 2 garlic cloves
- 110g / 4 oz dried brown rice

- 600ml / 20 fl oz gluten-free vegetable stock
- 50g / 1¾ oz broccoli florets
- 3 tbsp low fat soft cheese
- 2 tbsp chopped dill

Method

Slice the mushrooms and garlic and cut the onion into wedges.

Heat a non stick frying pan until hot and spray with the cooking oil. Fry the onion and mushrooms for 5 minutes, add the garlic and cook for another 2 minutes.

In another pan add the rice to the stock and bring to a simmer. Cover and cook for 15 minutes. Add the onions, mushrooms and garlic and then the broccoli, cook for a further 5 minutes or until the rice is cooked and the stock has been absorbed.

If the rice is not quite cooked, add a little more hot water. Stir in the chopped dill and soft cheese and season to taste.

Spicy Potato Wraps – 235 kcal

This is an easy dish that won't need much shopping for. You will most likely have most of the ingredients in your cupboard already.

Serves 4 – 235 calories per serving
***Suitable for freezing
Preparation - 10 minutes
Cooking - 30 minutes

- 2 tsp sunflower oil
- 1 onion
- 2 tbsp gluten-free curry powder (to your taste)
- 400g / 14 oz can chopped tomatoes
- 750g / 1lb 10oz potatoes
- 2 tbsp mango chutney
- 100g / 4oz low-fat natural yoghurt
- 1 tsp ready mixed mint sauce
- 8 gluten-free chapattis or wraps.

Method

Slice the onion and peel and dice the potatoes into bite sized chunks.

Heat the oil and fry the sliced onion for 8 minutes until just soft. Add 1½ tablespoons of the curry powder and cook for about 30 seconds only.

Add the can of tomatoes and season well. Bring to a

simmer and cook without a lid for 15 minutes.

Meanwhile put the potatoes and the remaining ½ tablespoon of curry powder into a pan of boiling water and cook for 7 minutes or until just soft. Drain but keep 100ml / 3½ fl oz of the potato liquid. Add the potatoes, mango chutney and the liquid to the tomato sauce and heat through.

Mix together the mint sauce and yogurt, warm the chapattis or wraps as directed on the pack.

To serve just divide the mixture into 4 portions and divide 1 portion between 2 chapattis or wraps. Spoon some yogurt relish on top, roll up and enjoy.

Freeze the remaining portions if applicable and just defrost and heat through when required. The yogurt relish can also be frozen or made fresh again next time.

Spinach & Mushroom Stew - 210 kcal

This is truly one of the most delicious low calorie meals I cook. The wholegrain mustard gives it a real kick and I could eat this every day, even on my non fasting days. It is so filling that I can't believe the calorie count on the amount of filling.

Serves 2 – 210 calories per serving
***Suitable for freezing
Preparation - 15 minutes
Cooking - 40 minutes

- 200g / 8oz baby spinach or frozen spinach blocks
- 1 tbsp olive oil
- 250g / 10oz mixed small mushrooms such as chestnut / button / shitake
- 1 garlic clove
- 125ml / 4 fl oz gluten-free vegetable stock

- 175g / 6oz cooked new potatoes
- 1 tbsp gluten-free wholegrain mustard
- 1 tsp grated nutmeg
- 1 heaped tbsp reduced fat crème fraîche
- 150g / 6oz each of green beans and broccoli

Method

Heat oven to 200° C / 180° C fan / Gas Mark 6

Quarter the mushrooms, crush the garlic, and cut the cooked potatoes into bite size chunks. Wilt spinach in a colander by pouring a kettle of boiling water over it. .

Heat the oil in a large frying pan and cook the mushrooms on a high heat until slightly browned.

Add the crushed garlic and cook for another minute. Add the stock, nutmeg, mustard and potatoes, bring to the boil and simmer for a couple of minutes until reduced slightly.

If using frozen spinach blocks add at this stage and cook until spinach has defrosted. Remove from the heat and season with salt and freshly ground black pepper.

Add the crème fraîche and fresh wilted spinach if using and mix well. Reheat and serve at once with the steamed green beans and broccoli.

Sweet Potato Curry Wraps - 280 kcal

This curry dish is very satisfying as you can have a wrap or chapatti. This serves 4 so make sure you freeze the other portions for a quick lunch or supper.

Serves 4 – 280 calories per serving
***Suitable for freezing
Preparation - 10 minutes
Cooking - 25 minutes

- 300g / 10 oz sweet potato
- 400g /14 oz tin Italian plum tomatoes
- 400g / 14 oz tin gluten-free chickpeas
- 1 tsp dried chilli flakes
- 2 tbsp gluten-free curry paste
- 100g / 4 oz baby spinach fresh or frozen
- 4 tbsp fat free yogurt or sour cream

to serve - 1 gluten-free chapatti per serving

Method

Peel and cube the sweet potato and drain the chickpeas.

Cook the sweet potato for 10-12 minutes until tender. While the potato are doing cook the tomatoes, chickpeas, curry paste and chilli flakes for about 5 minutes at a gentle simmer, stirring often. Drain the potato and add to the tomato mix. Stir in the spinach and cook until wilted or until the frozen spinach is heated through.

Warm through the chapatti as instructed for about 30 seconds, add the filling and a spoonful of the yogurt, fold up and enjoy.

Vegetable & Bean Stew – 270 kcal

A warm and filling vegetable stew or hearty soup that is very quick to make.

Serves 2 - 270 calories per portion
Preparation - 10 minutes
Cooking - 20 minutes

- 1 onion
- 2 sticks celery
- 1 large leek
- 5oz frozen peas
- 400g / 14 oz tin gluten-free cannellini beans
- 500ml / 16 fl oz / 1 pint gluten-free vegetable stock
- 200g / 7 oz greens (either Spring greens, Sweetheart or Savoy cabbage)

Method

Split the leek in half length ways and wash under running water to remove any soil.

Roughly chop the onion, celery and leek and cook in a little oil until softened. Add the stock and drained beans and cook for about 4 minutes.

Add the greens or cabbage and cook for a further 5-8 minutes. If using Savoy Cabbage, cook until cabbage is as you like it perhaps a further 5-10 minutes according to taste.

Sprinkle with a little lemon juice and serve.

FISH

Baked Curried Cod – 246 kcal

This is a very economical and easy to cook dish and you can also use Monkfish or any other white chunky fish. You could also try it with thick salmon fillets

Serves 2 – 246 calories per serving
Preparation - 20 minutes
Cooking - 40 minutes

- 1 tsp oil
- 300g / 11 oz cod fillet or other firm fish
- 50g / 2 oz fresh gluten-free white breadcrumbs
- 1 tbsp blanched almonds
- 2 tsp gluten-free Thai green curry paste
- 1 lime
- 100g / 4 oz mixed salad or rocket leaves
- 2 tomatoes
- 2 garlic cloves
- Dribble olive oil

Method

Pre-heat the oven to 200C or 400F or Gas mark 6

Divide the cod fillet into 2 equal portions and place in a single layer in a shallow oven-proof dish that has been brushed with the oil.

Chop the almonds and mix together with the grated rind of ½ a lime, green curry paste and the breadcrumbs. Stir thoroughly to blend them all in and season with salt and pepper.

Top the fish with the paste, carefully patting onto the top of the fillets and around the sides so that the fish is well covered. Bake in the pre-heated oven for 35-40 minutes or until the fish is cooked and the top is crusty and brown.

Once the fish is cooking, cut the tomatoes in half and place in a shallow oven proof dish. Peel and slice the garlic cloves and push slivers into the tomato flesh, dribble with the olive oil and bake for 15 minutes, timed to finish with the fish.

Serve with the green salad and the juices from the fish and tomatoes.

Fishcakes & Tomato Sauce – 290 kcal

You can make these fishcakes using a combination of any white fish and fresh salmon or you can just use one type of fish. Make them ahead of time as they need to chill for at least an hour before cooking.

serves 2 - 290 calories per serving
***Suitable for freezing
Preparation - 15 minutes plus 1 hour chilling
Cooking - 10-15 minutes

- 225g / 8 oz potatoes
- 225g / 8 oz any white or mixture of fish fillet
- 200ml / 7 fl oz or 1 cup gluten-free fish stock
- 1 tbsp low-fat fromage frais
- 2 tbsp fresh chives
- 40g / 1½ oz dry fresh gluten-free white or brown breadcrumbs
- 1 lemon, cut into wedges

Sauce
- 100m / 3½ fl oz / ⅓ cup gluten-free passata or sieved tomatoes
- 2 tbsp low-fat fromage frais
- Smoked paprika

Method

Peel and dice the potatoes and cook in boiling water for 10 minutes or until soft. Drain and mash.

Place fish in the stock, bring to the boil and poach on low heat for about 8 minutes. Make sure fish is cooked through and then remove from stock and break into flakes, discarding the skin.

Very carefully, mix together the mashed potato, flaked fish, fromage frais, snipped chives and salt & pepper. Leave the mixture to cool, cover and chill for at least 1 hour.

Divide the mixture into 4 parts and make each portion into a round patty type fishcake. Put the breadcrumbs onto a plate and press the fishcakes into the crumbs until it is covered all over.

Fry the fishcakes in the oil for about 6 minutes each side or until golden and crisp. When ready, drain on kitchen paper and keep warm in a low oven.

Make the sauce by gently heating the passata and when hot but not boiling, remove from heat, stir in the fromage frais and the smoked paprika to taste and serve with the fishcakes and lemon wedges on a bed of green lettuce or green beans

Mussels in White Wine – 278 kcal

Use the freshest muscles you can find for this dish and it won't disappoint. You really should have some crusty French bread to mop up the juices but if you have this dish on one of your fasting days, that would tip you over your allowance. Save the juice for the next day and have it for lunch with the bread.

Serves 2 – 278 calories per serving
Preparation - 30 minutes
Cooking - 25 minutes

- 1 kg / 2¼ lbs of live mussels
- 2 tbsp olive oil
- 2-4 large garlic cloves, halved
- 400g / 14 oz tin chopped tomatoes
- 150ml / 5 fl oz / ⅔ cup of white wine

- 1 tbsp finely chopped fresh leaf parsley
- 2 tsp finely chopped fresh oregano

Method

Soak the live mussels in a bowl of lightly salted water for an hour. Rinse under cold running water and remove any sand by rubbing them lightly with a soft brush. Using a sharp knife remove any 'beards' from the shells.

Throw out any broken shells or any that are open and don't close if tapped firmly with a knife handle. These are dead and must not be eaten as they can cause food poisoning.

Rinse the mussels again, drain and put to one side in a colander.

Heat the oil over a medium heat in a large pan and sauté the garlic for about 2 minutes but be careful not to burn it and then remove from the pan.

Add the tomatoes and juices, wine and herbs and bring to a simmer. Lower the heat and simmer for about 5 minutes.

Tip the mussels into the sauce, cover and simmer for 5-7 minutes, making sure you shake the pan often until all the mussels have opened.

Lift the mussels from the pan with a slotted spoon, removing any that have not opened and discard them, spoon into warmed bowls.

Season the sauce to taste and pour over the mussels, top with extra finely chopped parsley.

Prawn and Chilli Wrap – 240 kcal

This is a very quick dish to make and the sweet chilli sauce really livens up what could potentially be a bland wrap.

Serves 1 - 240 calories per serving
Preparation - 2 minutes

- 1 gluten-free wrap
- 40g / 1½ oz shredded lettuce any kind you like
- 75g / 3 oz cooked prawns
- ½ chopped tomato
- 1 tbsp gluten-free sweet chilli sauce

Method

Mix the prawns with the chilli sauce. Spread the lettuce over the wrap, making sure you leave a gap clear at the bottom for folding up. Also spread the prawn mixture evenly over the lettuce and then sprinkle the chopped tomato on the top.

Fold up the bottom flap and then roll the remaining wrap gently taking care not to split the folds. It helps if you can warm your wrap in the oven first as it will be more pliable.

Prawn and Dill Soup – 250 kcal

A delicious and filling soup that is substantial enough to be called a stew.

serves 2 - 250 calories per serving
***Suitable for freezing
Preparation - 5 minutes
Cooking - 10 minutes

- 750ml / 1½ pints / 3 cups gluten-free chicken stock
- 2 tbsp gluten-free fish sauce
- 1 thumb sized piece fresh ginger
- 150g / 5 oz cooked basmati rice
- juice of 1 lime
- 3 plum tomatoes
- 150g / 5 oz raw or cooked prawns
- 15g/ ¾ oz chopped dill

Method

Peel and shred the ginger and de-seed and chop the tomatoes.

In a medium pan, bring the stock to a boil and add the fish sauce, shredded ginger, lime juice, chopped tomatoes, dill, prawns and the rice.

Simmer for a few minutes until the prawns are cooked. If using cooked prawns only cook until they are heated through otherwise they will start to shrink and go hard.

Serve in heated bowls with a sprinkling of coriander if liked (optional)

Tuna & Salmon Kebabs – 355 kcal

Tuna steak meat is ideal for threading on to sticks for kebabs and cooks really well on either the grill or barbecue.

Serves 2 – 355 calories per serving
Preparation – 5 minutes + 10 minutes marinating
Cooking - 5 minutes

- 1 tuna & 1 salmon streak approx 125g / 4½ oz each
- 1 small courgette or zucchini
- 100g / 3½ oz gluten-free quinoa
- 2 tbsp gluten-free harrisa paste
- 2 lemons
- 200ml / 7oz / scant 1 cup gluten-free vegetable stock
- 1 tsp cumin
- small bunch mint, chopped

Method

Cut the tuna and salmon into fairly large chunks. Squeeze the juice from 1 lemon and cut the other into wedges for serving later. Mix the harissa paste with 1 tbsp lemon juice and coat the fish pieces with it. Leave to marinate for 10 minutes.

Bring the stock to the boil and add the cumin, stir and pour in the quinoa. Bring back to a boil, turn of the heat, cover and leave to stand for 5 minutes and then stir and fluff up.

Slice the courgette/zucchini into medium thickness slices diagonally into long pieces.

Thread the fish and vegetable slices alternately and evenly between 4 skewers and grill or barbecue for 2 minutes each side or until the fish is cooked through.

Mix the remaining lemon juice and mint and serve with the fish kebabs and the lemon wedges and a green salad or a big helping of steamed broccoli.

Salmon & Ginger Stir Fry – 295 kcal

serves 2 – 295 calories per portion
Preparation - 10 minutes
Cooking - 10-15 minutes

- 2 x 115g / 4½ oz salmon fillets
- 1 large head of broccoli
- 1 large carrot
- 115g / 4 oz mange tout
- 1 inch piece of fresh root ginger
- 2 tbsp gluten-free soy sauce
- 2 tsp vegetable oil
- ½ lemon, sliced

Method

Wash the salmon, check for any stray bones and drain on kitchen paper.

Prepare the vegetables by breaking or slicing the broccoli into small florets. Peel the carrot and cut into dice and slice the mange tout into strips, cutting off the top and bottom first. Peel the fresh ginger and again slice into matchstick size strips. Put all the vegetables into a large bowl and mix in 1 tbsp soy sauce, put to one side.

Preheat a grill or barbecue and place the salmon on the grill pan, brush with the other half of the soy sauce and grill for 2-3 minutes each side depending on the thickness of the fillet or until cooked through.

In the meantime, heat the oil in a wok or large frying pan and stir fry the vegetables for about 5 minutes on medium heat until cooked through or to taste. When vegetables are cooked divide between 2 warmed plates and serve the fish on top with a lemon slice and a dash of soy sauce.

Tuna Curry Broth 239 kcal

This soup is made using tinned tuna and can be made quickly or in advance and makes a really filling lunch or dinner.

Serves 4 – 239 calories per serving
***Suitable for freezing
Preparation - 10 minutes
Cooking - 50-60 minutes

- 200g / 7 oz tin tuna in spring water
- 25g / 1 oz butter
- 1 medium onion
- 1 clove garlic
- 2 tbsp gluten-free curry paste
- 400g / 14 oz tin plum tomatoes
- 3 tbsp white rice

- 1 small courgette
- 125ml / 4 fl oz / ½ cup single cream

Method

Finely chop the onion and garlic clove and wash and finely dice the courgette. Drain the tuna but reserve the water and make up to 600ml or 2½ cups with boiling water.

Melt the butter in a large pan and sauté the onion and garlic for 5minutes or until softened. Stir in the curry paste and cook off for 1 minute, stirring constantly.

Add the water mixture a little at a time stirring well and bring to a low simmer. Add the tomatoes, breaking up with the spoon, return to the boil, add the rice, cover and simmer gently for about 10 minutes.

Finally, add the tuna and courgette and cook for a further 15 minutes or until the courgette and rice are cooked.

Stir in the cream and adjust the seasoning to taste. Simmer for another 2-3 minutes to heat thoroughly and serve in warmed bowls.

Tuna Steaks & Beans – 250 kcal

This recipe is still one of our favourites because you can change the Tuna to almost any other meat or fish. Try is with fishcakes, salmon fillets, steak, chicken etc. The variations are endless.

Serves 2 - 250 calories per serving
Preparation - 5 minutes
Cooking - 10 minutes

- 2 x 100g / 4 oz tuna steaks
- 150g / 5 oz mixed salad leaves or rocket
- 400g / 14 oz gluten-free cannellini beans, drained & rinsed
- 2 or 3 garlic cloves, sliced
- bunch spring onions (scallions), sliced
- 1 tsp olive oil
- 2 tbsp lemon juice either fresh or bottled

Method

Cook tuna for a few minutes each side until cooked as you like it, or if using frozen cook according to packet instructions.

At the same time, in a small pan, sauté the garlic in the olive oil for a few seconds taking care not to burn it and then add the drained and rinsed beans and lemon juice.

Cook for a few more minutes and spoon over the arranged salad leaves. Sprinkle over the spring onions (scallions), drizzle some balsamic vinegar and serve with the Tuna steaks.

MEAT & POULTRY

Beef Strips with Pak Choy – 265 kcal

Pak Choy is used a lot in oriental cooking with good reason. It is low in calories and goes well with almost anything.

Serves 2 – 265 calories per serving
Preparation – 10 minutes
Cooking – 10 minutes

- 1 tbsp oil
- 1 large sirloin steak
- Small piece fresh ginger
- 1 garlic clove

- 4 spring onions (scallions)
- 1 tbsp gluten-free soy sauce
- 2 pak choy
- 50g / 2 oz mange tout or snow peas

Method

Trim all the fat off the steak and cut it into very thin slices. Peel and grate the ginger. Slice the spring onions (scallions). Crush the garlic. Cut the pak choy lengthways into quarters.

Heat the oil in a wok and brown the beef. When browned, add the ginger and onions and stir fry for 2 minutes. Add the soy sauce and keep warm.

Steam the pak choy and mange tout until tender, serve with the beef.

Beef with Green Lentils – 220 kcal

This is a variation on spaghetti bolognese that freezes really well. You can have this as a topping for a jacket potato, but do not eat the skin or your calories will rocket. Also have it with some steamed broccoli and courgettes which are very few calories.

Serves 6 – 220 calories per serving
***Suitable for freezing
Preparation – 5 minutes
Cooking – 40-45 minutes

- 400g / 14oz lean minced beef
- 1 large onion
- 1 tsp gluten-free wholegrain mustard
- 2 tbsp gluten-free soy sauce
- 2 tbsp gluten-free tomato puree
- 400g / 14 oz can chopped tomatoes
- 200g / 7 oz green lentils

Method

Peel and chop the onion and rinse the lentils in cold water, drain. Cook the mince and onion in a non-stick pan on a medium heat until the meat is brown all over, stirring often.

Add the mustard, some freshly ground black pepper and salt to taste. Next add the soy sauce, chopped tomatoes plus one can of water and finally the tomato puree. Stir to combine all the ingredients and bring to a low simmer. Stir in the rinsed lentils and cover and simmer for 30 minutes until sauce is nicely thickened.

Add some chopped chives if wished (optional) and serve with some steamed vegetables or a 200g / 7 oz jacket potato (add 154 calories) but don't eat the skin (or add another 118 calories).

Chicken, Apricot & Spinach – 250 kcal

Chicken and apricots go well together and make a nice change from the usual stuffings for chicken.

Serves 1 – 250 calories
Preparation – 10 minutes
Cooking – 25 minutes

- 1 skinless boneless chicken breast
- 1 small onion
- 1 garlic clove
- 2 tsp olive oil
- 2 dried apricots
- 50g / 2 oz spinach
- 2 tsp cumin
- 2 tsp clear honey

Method

Heat the oven to 200°C / fan 180°C / gas 6

Halve and thinly slice the onion and garlic. Finely chop the apricots and chop the spinach.

Sauté the onion and garlic in a frying pan with the oil for 5 minutes season well and add the apricots, spinach and 1 tsp cumin and cook for a further minute or two.

Make a cut in the chicken across the side to form a pocket and stuff the cooked mixture into the breast. Rub the remaining cumin into the top of the chicken and season.

Pour over the honey, put in a small dish and bake for 20 minutes until cooked. Serve with a portion of green beans or steamed broccoli.

Chicken & Cherry Tomatoes – 260 kcal

A very quick lunch or dinner meal that is easy to cook and delicious to eat.

serves 2 - 260 calories per serving
Preparation - 5 minutes
Cooking - 15 minutes

- 2 skinless boneless chicken breasts
- 1 tbsp seasoned gluten-free plain flour
- olive oil
- 1 medium onion
- 3 sticks celery
- 100g / 4 oz cherry or baby plum tomatoes
- 1 lemon
- 1 tbsp white wine vinegar
- 2 tbsp chopped basil leaves
- Rocket or baby salad leaves to serve.

Method

Halve and slice the onion, thinly slice the celery and halve the tomatoes.

Cut the chicken breasts in half to form 4 thin breasts. Place between 2 sheets of cling film and flatten a bit more using a suitable heavy object to form thin escallops without destroying the flesh.

Place the seasoned flour on a plate and dip the chicken breast in it to evenly coat, shake off any excess.

Heat the oil over a medium heat in a non stick frying pan and when hot, fry the chicken pieces until they are brown on both sides and cooked through.

Remove from the pan and add the celery and onion and fry for 4 minutes.

Next put in the tomatoes and cook for a further 4 minutes until starting to soften.

Add the vinegar and the chicken again and cook through for 3-4 minutes and then stir in the chopped basil. Serve with salad leaves of choice.

Chicken Parcels – 280 kcal

This is a very easy dish to prepare and cook. The chicken breast stays lovely and moist and the vegetables cook just right. As a bonus there will be very little washing up and even if you leave it longer in the oven, the flavours will just increase.

serves 1 - 280 calories
Preparation - 10 minutes
Cooking - 50-60 minutes

- 1 x Chicken Breast approx 125g / 4½ oz
- ½ medium onion sliced
- 1 small courgette or zucchini sliced
- 100g / 4 oz green beans cut into half
- 1 medium tomato sliced
- 75g / 3 oz broccoli florets

- 1 gluten-free chicken stock cube

Method

Make a parcel using foil or small roasting bag and place the vegetables in the foil or bag. Lay the chicken breast on top of the vegetables.

Make up the stock cube as directed and pour some onto the chicken parcels, not too much, just enough to keep the parcels moist.

Season well with salt and pepper. Add a tsp of your favourite dried herbs or a handful of fresh if you have them.

Fold up and seal the parcels, not too tightly or the heat won't penetrate and the vegetables won't cook through. Place the parcel in an oven proof dish and cook for a minimum of 50-60 minutes at 190c.

Chicken & Cabbage Broth – 250 kcal

This is a delicious, nutritious and filling broth that you can freeze and save for another fasting day or have it for lunch with some gluten-free bread on a normal day.

serves 4 - 250 calories per serving
***Suitable for freezing
Preparation - 10 minutes
Cooking - 20 - 25 minutes

- 1 litre / 1¾ pints / 4 cups gluten-free chicken stock
- 2 skinless chicken breasts
- 4 carrots
- 100g / 4 oz gluten-free casarecce or fusilli pasta
- ½ Savoy cabbage
- 3 spring onions (scallions)
- 2 tbsp gluten-free pesto

Method

Peel the carrots and cut into lengths. Core the cabbage and slice roughly. Top and tail the spring onions (scallions) and slice.

In a large pan, place the stock, chicken breasts and carrots, bring to a simmer and cook on a low heat for 5 minutes.

Add the pasta, cabbage, spring onions (scallions) and salt and pepper. Simmer for a further 5 minutes until the pasta is tender and the chicken is cooked through.

Using a ladle, remove the chicken from the pan and slice. Portion out the broth using a ladle into however many portions you are serving. Top with the sliced chicken and ½ tbsp of pesto per serving.

Chicken, Pea and Rice Soup – 290 kcal

I know this is a soup but the rice makes is a filling lunch or dinner meal. Try it because you should have the majority of ingredients in your store cupboard and can even use leftover chicken.

Serves 2 – 290 calories per serving
***Suitable for freezing
Preparation – 5 minutes
Cooking – 10-15 minutes

- 750ml / 1½ pts / 3¼ cups gluten-free chicken stock
- 50g / 2 oz long grain rice
- 1 cooked chicken breast or leftover chicken
- 50g / 2 oz defrosted frozen peas
- small handful basil leaves

Method

Heat the chicken stock in a medium pan, add the rice and cook for 8-10 minutes. Add the shredded chicken breast and peas and cook for a further 2 minutes. Season and add the torn basil leaves and serve.

Lamb and Apricot Casserole – 280 kcal

This is a fruity meat casserole with a bit of a kick. The lamb and apricots complement each other and the spices perk it all up. Again, plenty to freeze here.

Serves 4 – 280 calories per serving
***Suitable for freezing
Preparation – 10 minutes
Cooking – 1 hour 20 minutes

- 450g / 1 lb lean lamb
- 1 tsp ground cinnamon
- 1tsp ground coriander
- 1 tsp ground cumin
- 2 tsp olive oil

- 1 medium red onion
- 1 garlic clove
- 400g / 14oz tin chopped tomatoes
- 2 tbsp gluten-free tomato puree
- 125g / 4½ oz ready to eat dried apricots
- 1 tsp sugar
- 300ml / ½ pint / 1¼ cups gluten-free vegetable stock

Method

Pre-heat the oven to 180°C/350°F/Gas 4

Trim all fat from the meat and cut into 2.5cm/1 inch chunks. Finely chop the red onion and crush the garlic.

Put the meat into a bowl and mix in the spices and the oil. Make sure all of the pieces are coated well.

Heat a non-stick pan until it's hot and then add the lamb. Reduce the heat and cook stirring for 5 minutes until browned all over. Remove the lamb from the pan using a slotted spoon and put into a large ovenproof casserole.

Now cook the onions, garlic, tomatoes and puree for 5 minutes in the same pan, stirring in any juices left from the meat. Season to taste and add the whole apricots and sugar and then the stock and bring to the boil.

Remove from heat and spoon the mixture over the lamb in the casserole, cover and cook for 1 hour. Remove the lid and cook for another 10 minutes

Serve with steamed broccoli on a fasting day and rice on a normal day.

Pork Chilli with Beans – 294 kcal

A one pot dish that you will eat over and over again, it's that good. Use tenderloin of pork because it is a really tender cut of pork and such good value as there's no waste. Because this serves 4 this is another one for the freezer.

serves 4 - 294 calories per serving
***Suitable for freezing
Preparation - 10 minutes
Cooking - 30 - 35 minutes

- 1 tbsp olive oil
- 400g / 14 oz pork tenderloin
- 1 medium onion
- 2 garlic cloves
- good pinch chilli flakes or crushed chilli
- 1 tsp cumin
- 1 red bell pepper
- 1 400g / 14 oz can chopped tomatoes
- 400ml / 14 fl oz / 1½ cups gluten-free chicken stock
- 250g / 9 oz small salad potatoes
- 100g / 4 oz green beans

Method

Dice the pork into bite sized pieces. Halve and slice the onion and then peel and slice the garlic. De-seed the red pepper and cut into chunks. Wash and halve the salad potatoes.

Top and tail the green beans and cut in half.

Heat the oil in a large pan and when hot, season and brown the pork. When browned all over, remove from pan and add the onion and garlic and sauté for a minute.

Add the chilli, cumin and pepper and cook for a further 2 minutes. Put the pork back in the pan with the tomatoes and stock and bring to a simmer. Add the potatoes and cook for about 10-15 minutes, stirring occasionally until the potatoes and meat are tender.

Add the green beans and cook for a further 5 minutes. Season and serve.

Pork & Mixed Peppers – 285 kcal

Very quick and easy supper dish that can be served to family and guests with extra vegetables or new potatoes

Serves 2 – 285 calories per serving
Preparation - 10 minutes
Cooking - 30 minutes

- 2½ tbsp olive oil
- 1 small onion
- 2 cloves garlic
- 2 peppers, 1 red, 1 yellow
- 200g / 7 oz chopped tomatoes
- 2 pork escallops
- 1 tbsp red wine vinegar

Method

Finely chop the onion and de-seed and finely slice the peppers. Finely slice 1 garlic clove and crush the other. Trim the fat from the meat.

In a large frying pan, heat 1 tbsp olive oil and cook the onions for 5 minutes until soft. Add the sliced garlic and cook for a further minute. Add the peppers and 2 tbsp water and cover and cook for 10 minutes. Add the tomatoes and cook for 10-15 minutes uncovered until the peppers are soft.

Brush the pork with ½ tbsp of oil and grill or griddle for 3-5 minutes each side depending on taste. Leave to rest covered with foil.

Mix the remaining 1 tbsp olive oil and the vinegar with the crushed garlic. Make a bed of the pepper mixture on a warmed plate, top with the pork and drizzle over the dressing.

Serve with steamed broccoli if fasting or potatoes and vegetables if not.

Pork & Roasted Vegetables – 235 kcal

Simple dish to prepare and cook but filling nevertheless.

Serves 2 – 235 calories per serving
Preparation – 10 minutes
Cooking – 25-30 minutes

- 1 large carrot
- 1 red pepper
- 1 courgette
- 1 tbsp olive oil
- 2 good size pork chops
- ¼ tsp paprika
- 50g / 2 oz watercress

Method
Preheat the oven to 200°C / fan 180°C / Gas 6
  Peel and slice the carrot and slice the courgette. Deseed and chop the red pepper. Place in a roasting tin

and mix in the oil. Season and roast for 25-30 minutes.

Meantime, heat a grill or griddle pan. Sprinkle the pork chops with the paprika and cook for 5 minutes each side.

Remove the vegetables from the oven and stir in the watercress. Serve with the pork chop.

Spicy Chicken Pitta – 275 kcal

Serves 1 - 275 calories per serving
Preparation - 5 minutes
Marinating - 30 minutes
Cooking: 10m

- 2 spring onions (scallions), chopped finely
- 2 garlic cloves, chopped finely
- juice ½ lemon
- 1 tsp honey
- ½ tsp paprika
- ¼ tsp mild chilli powder

- ½ chicken breast fillet
- 1 gluten-free pitta bread or wrap
- small amount iceberg or other lettuce

Method

Finely chop the spring onion and garlic and mix together with the lemon juice, honey, paprika and chilli powder to form a marinade.

Cut the chicken breast into small lumps about 2.5cm or 1 inch square. Mix the chicken with the marinade and leave it in the fridge for at least 30 minutes, longer if possible.

Pre-heat your grill to the highest setting and when ready, grill the chicken for roughly 8 minutes, turning over half way through. The chicken pieces will be ready when nicely crisp and brown. Remove from grill and quickly toast your pita bread. Make a pocket in the pita and fill with the shredded lettuce and cooked chicken.

LESS THAN 400 CALORIES

These menus are less than or just 400 calories and are mostly suitable for your main meal whether that is lunch or dinner. These can often be interchanged with your choice of meat or fish.

VEGETARIAN

Baked Veggie Pasta - 385 kcal

This dish is so easy to make and is absolutely delicious. Even though it is for 4 you really should make it all and freeze the remainder because you will be eating it often.

Serves 4 – 385 calories per serving
***Suitable for freezing
Preparation - 15 minutes
Cooking - 40 - 50 minutes

- 1 small onion
- 2 garlic cloves
- 250g small chestnut mushrooms
- 400g / 14 oz tin chopped tomatoes
- 1 tbsp dried oregano
- 1 tsp mixed dried herbs
- 1 tbsp gluten-free tomato puree
- 150 ml / 5 fl oz gluten-free vegetable stock
- 125g / 4½ oz gluten-free fusilli or other small pasta shapes
- 300g / 10½ oz low fat soft cheese
- 2 egg yolks

Method

Preheat the oven to 180° C / 160° C fan / Gas 4

Grate the onion, crush the garlic and quarter the mushrooms. If mushrooms large just chop a bit smaller.

In a large bowl mix together the onion, garlic, mushrooms, tomatoes, oregano and tomato puree.

Stir the stock into the mixture and add the fresh pasta, season well. Turn into a 1½ litre / 2¾ pint oven-proof dish.

Mix the soft cheese and egg yolks together and season well. Spread over the top of the mince mixture and bake in the oven for 40-45 minutes.

Serve with a good portion of steamed broccoli.

Divide remaining portions and freeze as required. To re-heat from frozen just place in suitable oven proof container, cover with foil and bake for 20-25 minutes at 180C or until cooked through.

Butternut Squash Risotto – 365 kcal

Risotto is a very easy dish to master once you get the hang of it. This recipe serves 2 but it freezes well so cook bigger batches so that you can have more ready meals in the freezer.

Serves 2 – 365 calories per serving
***Suitable for freezing
Preparation – 10 minutes
Cooking – 20-25 minutes

- 1 small onion
- 1 tbsp olive oil
- 1 x 250g / 9 oz butternut squash
- 150g / 5 oz carnaroli or arborio risotto rice
- 600ml / 1¼ pint / 2½ cups gluten-free vegetable stock
- 2 tbsp grated parmesan

Method

Chop the onion finely. Peel and dice the butternut squash or pumpkin.

Heat the oil in a large pan and fry the onion until softened. Add the rice and stir until coated in the oil. Add the squash and half the hot stock and stir well. Cook, stirring often until most of the stock has been absorbed. Then add a little stock at a time, again stirring until absorbed.

Repeat this until all the stock has been used and the rice and squash are cooked. The rice should have a little bite but not grainy. Add more stock or hot water if needed.

Add the cheese to the rice and stir well. Cover the pan and leave to sit for 1 minute.

Season well and dish out into warmed bowls

Fresh Pesto with Pasta – 365 kcal

This sauce is can be cooked in bigger batches and kept in the freezer for a very quick meal. It can be used from frozen so no need to defrost first.

Makes 6 – 8 servings of pesto sauce
365 calories per serving including pasta
***Pesto Sauce Suitable for freezing
Preparation - 10 minutes
Cooking -15 minutes

Pesto Sauce
- 100g / 4oz mixed soft herbs such as basil, mint, chives, dill etc.
- 300 ml / 10 fl oz / ½ pint full fat crème fraîche
- 100g /4oz grated parmesan cheese
- 100g / 4oz toasted pine nuts

To serve per person
- 2 tbsp pesto sauce (as above)
- 50g / 2oz gluten-free spaghetti or other favourite pasta per person

Method

Put the herbs, crème fraîche and cheese in food processor and mix together. Add the pine nuts and mix a little more until slightly chopped but not smooth.

Season with plenty and I mean plenty of salt and freshly ground pepper. Divide pesto between small pots allowing 2 tablespoons per serving and freeze portions you are not using.

Cook the pasta as directed on packet, drain well and just stir in the fresh pesto sauce. If using frozen pesto, when pasta is cooked and drained as above, put the frozen block of pesto in the bottom of the pan and tip the pasta on top.

Cover pan and leave to sit for 10 minutes and then stir the pesto through the pasta. Top with a little more parmesan cheese and a handful of herbs if liked.

Golden Rice & Red Onions – 365 kcal

This dish has a hint of Indian spices and the turmeric gives the rice a warming yellow colour. Leave the topping onions out if not to your taste or too much bother to do but they do add a little more colour and flavour.

Serves 2 – 365 per portion
***Suitable for freezing
Preparation - 10 minutes
Cooking - 25-30 minutes

- 90g / 3½ oz basmati rice
- 30g / 1 oz red lentils
- 1 bay leaf
- 3 cardamom pods, split
- 1 tsp ground turmeric
- 3 whole cloves
- ½ tsp cumin seeds

- ½ cinnamon stick
- 1 small onion
- 125g / 4½ oz cauliflower florets
- 1 medium carrot
- 50g / 2 oz frozen peas
- 30g / 1 oz sultanas
- 300ml / 10 fl oz / 1¼ cups gluten-free vegetable stock
- 1 tbsp chopped fresh coriander (optional)

For the Onions
- 1 tsp vegetable oil
- 1 small red onion
- 1 small white onion
- 1 tsp caster sugar

Method

Peel and dice the carrot, break the cauliflower into small florets. Put the carrot, cauliflower, onion, rice, lentils, spices, bay leaf, peas and sultanas into a large pan. Season and thoroughly mix.

Pour over the stock, bring to the boil, cover and simmer for 15 minutes stirring occasionally to avoid the rice sticking. Add more stock if it runs dry before the rice is cooked

When the rice is tender, remove, cover and it let stand for about 10 minutes or until all the liquid has been absorbed. Take out the bay leaf, cardamom pods, cloves and cinnamon stick.

While the rice is cooking, shred the onions, heat the oil in a frying pan and fry the onions over a medium heat for 4 minutes until just starting to soften.

Add the sugar, turn up the heat and cook, stirring all the time for a further 2-3 minutes until golden but not burnt.

Stir the rice mixture through and serve on warmed plates with the onions on top and sprinkled with the chopped coriander if liked.

Leek and Mushroom Bake - 330 kcal

Serves 2 – 330 calories per serving
Preparation - 20 minutes
Cooking - 50 minutes

- 6 medium open or Portobello mushrooms
- 2 garlic cloves
- 2 medium leeks
- 400g / 14 oz tin chopped tomatoes
- 1 tsp mixed dried herbs
- 1 tbsp gluten-free tomato puree

For the crumble
- 50g / 1¾ oz gluten-free plain white flour
- 25g / 1 oz gluten-free porridge oats
- ½ tsp English mustard powder
- 15g / ½ oz low fat spread
- 50g / 1¾ oz half fat Cheddar cheese

Method

Preheat the oven to 190° / 170° C fan / Gas 5

Halve and thickly slice the mushrooms and the leeks. Peel and crush the garlic.

Stir fry the mushrooms and leeks for 5 minutes in an oiled frying pan. Add the garlic and cook for a further 2 minutes.

Add the tomatoes, tomato puree, herbs and seasoning and simmer for 10 minutes.

For the topping, mix together the flour, oats, mustard powder and low fat spread and rub together until it resembles breadcrumbs.

Add the cheese and season to taste.

Place the mushroom and leek mixture in an oven proof casserole dish and cover with the crumb mixture. Cook in the oven for about 30 minutes or until the crumble is crisp and browned.

Serve with a big portion of steamed broccoli.

Low Fat Pesto Tagliatelle – 350 kcal

Pesto sauce is quite high in fat content but this sauce uses fromage frais instead of oil and is therefore much healthier. You can also use any colour pasta you choose or try a combination of green and white tagliatelli.

Serves 2 – 350 calories per portion
***Suitable for freezing
Preparation - 10 minutes
Cooking - 15 minutes

- 125g / 4½ oz chestnut or other mixed mushrooms
- 75ml / 3 oz / ⅓ cup vegetable stock
- 90g / 3½ oz asparagus
- 150g / 5 oz gluten-free tagliatelle or spaghetti
- 200g / 7 oz ready to eat artichoke hearts
- Parmesan shavings

Pesto sauce
- 1 garlic clove
- 15g / ½ oz fresh basil leaves
- 3 tbsp low-fat natural fromage frais
- 1 tbsp grated Parmesan cheese

Method

Make the pesto sauce by either using a blender or finely chopping the basil and mixing it well with all the other ingredients.

To make the pasta, slice the mushrooms, place in a small pan with the stock, bring to the boil and poach in the vegetable stock for 4 minutes. Drain and set aside.

Rinse out the pan, trim and cut the asparagus into 5cm (2") lengths and cook in boiling water for 3-4 minutes, drain and also set aside.

Cook the pasta as directed on the packet, drain, sprinkle with a little olive oil to stop it sticking, return to the pan. Add the mushrooms, cooked asparagus, and the drained and halved artichoke hearts and cook on a very low heat for about 2 minutes.

Remove from heat and stir in the pesto sauce and serve with a few shredded basil leaves and the parmesan shavings.

Mixed Vegetable Bake – 330 kcal

This is a substantial vegetable dish with a potato and cheese topping. This is unusual for a low calorie meal so enjoy it. You can also make individual portions for the freezer.

Serves 4 – 330 calories per serving
***Suitable for freezing
Preparation – 10 minutes
Cooking – 25-30 minutes

- 2 medium onions
- 1 garlic clove
- 1 red pepper
- 1 green pepper
- 1 medium aubergine
- 2 medium courgettes (zucchini)
- 2 x 400g /14oz tins chopped tomatoes
- ½ tbsp dried mixed herbs

- 2 tbsp gluten-free tomato puree
- 900g / 2lb potatoes
- 75g / 2¾ oz grated low fat cheese

Method

Finely chop the onions and garlic. Deseed and halve and slice the peppers. Top and tail the aubergine and cut into small chunks. Trim and thinly slice the courgettes.

Put the onion, garlic, peppers, dried herbs, tomato puree and the 2 tins of chopped tomatoes in a large pan. Bring to the boil, cover and simmer gently for 10 minutes, stirring occasionally.

Stir in the aubergine and courgettes and cook uncovered for another 10 minutes, giving it the occasional stir.

While the vegetables are cooking, peel and cut the potatoes into 2.5cm / 1 inch pieces. Boil them for 7-10 minutes until cooked through and then drain.

Put the vegetables into ovenproof dishes, depending on your chosen portion size. Place the potatoes on top of the vegetable mixture, dividing equally if using smaller dishes. Sprinkle the cheese on top of the potatoes.

Freeze your other portions at this stage.

Preheat your grill to medium and grill the dish for 5 minutes until the cheese is bubbling and the potatoes are getting golden and crispy. Serve on warmed plates with nothing else.

Mushroom Risotto – 365 kcal

Risotto is a really easy dish to cook once you get into the swing of it. You can use any variety of mushrooms you like.

Serves 1 - 365 calories
***Suitable for freezing
Preparation - 5-10 minutes
Cooking - 20-25 minutes

- 1 small onion
- 125g / 4½ oz mixed mushrooms
- 1 tsp olive oil
- 80g / 3 oz risotto rice
- 250ml / 8 fl oz / 1 cup hot gluten-free vegetable stock
- 20g / 1 oz Parmesan cheese, grated
- small handful of flat leaved parsley, chopped
- salt and black pepper

Method

Chop the onions and garlic, and wipe the mushrooms before also chopping them. Warm the oil in a large pan, add the onions and garlic and cook gently for 2 minutes. Then add the mixed mushrooms and cook for another minute or so.

Add the risotto rice and stir well to coat the rice with the juices for about a minute. Add enough of the hot stock to cover the rice and cook, stirring constantly until the liquid has been absorbed. Then add more hot stock and allow it to be absorbed also, (for best results you should keep the stock hot in a separate pan on the stove).

Repeat this process, stirring as you do, until the rice is ready, there should be a hint of grain but not too hard. Add more boiling water if necessary when stock has been used up.

Remove from heat, stir in the Parmesan and chopped parsley, check the seasoning and allow to stand for 1 minute before serving on warmed plates.

Mushrooms & Mustard Mash - 390 kcal

Mushrooms are a filling and tasty main dish and when served with this polenta mash you will have a substantial evening meal.

Serves 2 – 390 calories per serving
Preparation - 10 minutes
Cooking - 15 minutes

- 600ml / 20 fl oz gluten-free vegetable stock
- 1 tsp cornflour
- 1 small onion
- 2 garlic cloves
- 250g / 9 oz chestnut mushrooms
- 125ml / 4 fl oz red wine
- 2 tbsp gluten-free cranberry sauce
- 100g / 3½ oz dried quick cook Polenta
- 2 tsp gluten-free wholegrain mustard

- 30g / 1¼ oz grated mature cheese

Method

Finely chop the onion, crush the garlic and thickly slice the mushrooms.

Bring 400ml / 14 fl oz of the vegetable stock to the boil and blend the cornflour with the remaining 200ml / 6 fl oz.

Spray a non stick pan and fry the garlic, onions and mushrooms for about 5 minutes. Add the red wine and cook for a further minute.

Slowly add the remaining cornflour stock and the cranberry sauce. Cook gently for 2 minutes until nice and thick, season to taste and remove from heat and keep warm.

Once the stock is boiling, slowly add the Polenta, stir and cook for 1-2 minutes until thickened. Stir in the mustard and cheese and serve straight away with the mushrooms and sauce.

Pasta with Cherry Tomatoes - 325 kcal

A low fat recipe that is quite filling as well as being tasty and very quick and easy to make

Serves 1 - 325 calories
Preparation - 5 minutes
Cooking - 15 minutes

- 100g / 4 oz cherry tomatoes
- 3 black olives
- 1 clove of garlic, peeled
- A handful of basil
- 2 tsp olive oil
- 75g / 3 oz gluten-free whole-wheat pasta
- bag mixed salad leaves or rocket

Method

Chop the tomatoes, olives and garlic. Put them into a bowl with some basil, then drizzle with the oil and stir well.

Cook the pasta as directed. Once the pasta is cooked, drain and rinse through with boiling water and return to the pan.

Add the tomato mixture from the bowl and stir over a very low heat. Season well with and freshly ground black pepper, and serve immediately with a big helping of mixed salad leaves.

Penne with Pepper Sauce – 375 kcal

Pasta makes a filling supper dish but don't have it too often with meat. This only uses vegetables so is very healthy.

Serves 2 - 375 calories
***Suitable for freezing
Preparation - 15 minutes
Cooking - 20 minutes

- 1 red and 1 yellow pepper
- 1 medium red onion
- 2 cloves of garlic
- 1 tsp oil
- 175g / 6 oz gluten-free whole-wheat penne pasta

Method

Halve the peppers and remove the seeds and membranes. Rub the skins with a little olive oil and place them, skin sides up, on a piece of foil under a hot grill. Once the skins have burnt and turned brown, remove from grill and allow cool slightly. Pull off the skin, slice and put into a small mixing bowl.

Chop the onion and garlic. Cook the pasta as directed on the pack. While the pasta is cooking, put the oil in a large frying pan and gently fry the onion and garlic. Add the peppers and juices from the bowl and continue cooking, stirring them together. Add some pasta liquid to keep the sauce moist if necessary.

When the pasta is cooked, drain and return it to the pan. Add the pepper sauce, salt and lots of black pepper. Stir thoroughly and serve.

Sweetcorn Soufflé - 325 kcal

Don't be nervous about cooking a soufflé you will be surprised how easy they are to make and this dish has only a few ingredients.

Serves 2 – 325 calories per serving
Preparation - 12 minutes
Cooking - 60 minutes

- 2 eggs
- 25g / 1 oz gluten-free plain flour
- 1 tsp xanthan gum
- 200ml / 7 fl oz skimmed milk
- 200g / 7oz tin sweetcorn
- 60g / 2oz half fat cheddar cheese
- ½ green pepper

Method

Preheat the oven to 180°C / 160° C fan / Gas 4

Very lightly oil (or use a low calorie spray) a 700ml / 1¼ pint soufflé dish or 2 smaller individual dishes. Whisk together the eggs and flour and the xanthan gum then slowly whisk in the milk a little at a time.

When combined, stir in the drained sweetcorn, grated cheese and de-seeded and chopped green pepper, season to taste.

Pour mixture into the prepared soufflé dish or individual dishes and bake for 1 hour until puffed up and nicely browned but not burnt. The smaller dishes will only take about 45 minutes.

Serve with steamed broccoli and courgettes.

Tofu with Noodles - 385 kcal

Tofu is very low in fat and will absorb flavours if you marinate it long enough. Just make sure you cook with plenty of spices and herbs

Serves 2 – 385 calories per serving
Preparation - 10 minutes + 1 hour marinating
Cooking - 15 minutes

- 100g / 3½ oz firm tofu
- 1 tbsp gluten-free soy sauce
- 2½ cm / 1 inch piece fresh ginger
- 2 garlic cloves
- 40g / 1½ oz dried gluten-free rice noodles
- 150g / 5½oz frozen spinach
- 2 spring onions (scallions) or scallions
- 1 tsp sesame oil
- 1 tsp sesame seeds
- ½ tsp dried chilli flakes

Method

Drain and cube the tofu, peel and finely grate the ginger, crush the garlic, chop the frozen spinach and the spring onions (scallions).

Marinate the Tofu by placing in a small bowl and adding the soy sauce, ginger and garlic and mix together. Leave for about an hour or more if possible.

When Tofu is ready, cook the noodles in a large pan according to the packet instructions until soft.

Lightly oil a wok or large frying pan and add the spinach and spring onions (scallions) and stir fry for a couple of minutes until tender and thoroughly defrosted if using frozen spinach.

Add the tofu and marinade to the pan, toss in the noodles, sesame oil and seeds and turn gently until the tofu is heated through. Sprinkle over the chilli flakes and some coriander or parsley if liked.

Vegetable Stew & Dumplings - 315 kcal

You can use any seasonal or favourite vegetables for this dish. The dumplings give it a really satisfying feeling.

Serves 4 – 315 calories per serving
***Suitable for freezing
Preparation - 15 minutes
Cooking - 45 minutes

- 1 tsp oil
- 90g / 3¼ oz shallots or small onions
- 1 medium leek
- 225g / 8 oz parsnips
- 1 large carrot
- 1.2 ltrs / 2 pints gluten-free vegetable stock
- 25g / 1oz quinoa
- 400g tin gluten-free cannellini beans

- 150g / 5 oz small cauliflower florets
- handful of chopped parsley
- 90g / 3¼ oz gluten-free self raising flour
- 1 tsp ground coriander
- 1 tsp cumin seeds
- 2 tbsp low fat spread

Method

Halve the shallots or small onions, slice and thoroughly wash the leek, peel and slice the carrot and peel and chop the parsnips.

Make the dumplings by sifting the flour and cumin powder into a large bowl. Add the cumin seeds and rub in the low fat spread until all combined. Add a small amount of water, just enough to make a soft dough. Make into 8 dumplings and set aside.

Heat the oil in a large saucepan and fry the onions, leek, carrot and parsnip for about 6 minutes until soft but not browned.

Add the stock, quinoa and beans and bring to the boil. Reduce heat, cover pan and simmer for 20 minutes. Add the cauliflower and stir, then place the dumplings on top of the stew, cover and simmer gently for a further 20 minutes or until the dumplings are cooked through.

Season to taste and sprinkle over the parsley. Serve or freeze at this point giving 2 dumplings to each portion.

Vegetable & Tofu Stew - 345 kcal

This is a really lovely stew with a deep rich flavour. Make a bigger batch and freeze portions for another day, well worth the effort.

Serves 2 – 345 calories per serving
***Suitable for freezing
Preparation - 10 minutes
Cooking - 50 minutes

- 1 tsp oil
- 1 onion
- 300g / 10 oz firm tofu
- 50g / 2 oz dried apricots
- 30g / 1 oz sun-dried tomatoes
- 400g / 14oz tin chopped tomatoes
- 400g / 14 oz potatoes

- 1 large sweet potato
- 2 handfuls baby spinach

Method

Finely chop the onion and chilli. Roughly chop the tomatoes. Peel and cube the sweet potato and shred the baby spinach.

Put the lentils, stock, onion, tomatoes, spices and the red chilli into a pan, bring to a simmer and cook for 10 minutes. Add the sweet potato and cook for a further 10 minutes or until done. Stir in the shredded baby spinach and season to taste. When spinach is wilted, serve at once.

FISH

Fruity Fish Kebabs – 335 kcal

Any firm fish can be used to make these skewers but the combination of white and pink make the taste and look something special. You could also try it with tuna for a meatier taste.

Serves 2 – 335 calories per serving
Preparation - 15- 20 minutes
Cooking - 7-10 minutes

- 250g / 9 oz firm white fish such as Monkish or Cod
- 250g / 9 oz thick salmon fillet
- 1 large orange

- 1 small grapefruit
- fresh bay leaves

For the marinade
- 1 tsp grated lemon rind
- 2 tbsp lemon juice
- 1 tsp runny honey
- 1 garlic clove

Method

Crush the garlic and mix with the lemon juice, rind and honey and set aside. Skin the fish and cut into 8 pieces each type making 16 pieces in all.

Using a knife, remove the peel and pith from the grapefruit and orange and carefully cut out each segment. Try to make sure you have cut out all pith and linking membranes.

Thread 4 skewers alternating the two fish types, bay leaves, grapefruit and orange segments. Place the skewers in a long shallow dish or plate and pour over the marinade you made earlier. Cover and chill for a couple of hours, turning them over in the marinade every so often.

To cook, preheat a grill to medium heat, place a piece of foil on the grill pan or barbecue and grill for about 8 minutes, turning half way through. Make sure the fish is fully cooked.

Serve with a fresh green salad and baby tomatoes.

Olive and Anchovy Pasta – 365 kcal

This is very quick and simple meal and you can use any pasta with the sauce. Tagliatelli or spaghetti will work best because the sauce will stick to it for a more enjoyable taste.

Serves 2 – 365 calories per serving
***Suitable for freezing
Preparation - 20 minutes
Cooking - 30 minutes

- 2 tbsp olive oil
- 1 small red onion
- 2 anchovy fillets
- pinch chilli flakes
- 1 garlic clove

- 200g / 7 oz can chopped tomatoes
- 1 tbsp gluten-free tomato puree
- 115g / 4¼ oz gluten-free tagliatelli or other pasta
- 15g / ½ oz each of green and black pitted olives
- 1 tbsp capers
- 2 sun-dried tomatoes

Method

Finely chop the onion and garlic. Roughly chop or slice the olives and sun-dried tomatoes. Drain the anchovies and drain and rinse the capers.

Heat the oil in a pan and sauté the onion, anchovies and chilli flakes for 10 minutes until starting to turn brown, add the garlic and cook for a further 30 seconds. Add the canned tomatoes and puree and bring to a simmer and cook on a low heat for about 10 minutes.

In the meantime, cook the pasta as directed on pack until al-dente or firm but not hard.

Add the olives, sun-dried tomatoes and capers to the sauce. Simmer for a further 3 minutes and then season to taste.

Drain the pasta, return to the pan and add the sauce, stirring until pasta and sauce are fully combined. Serve at once.

Tuna Steak & Mash – 325 kcal

Sweet Potato is actually slightly higher in calories and carbs than white potatoes so you can have either. Personally I prefer the taste of the sweet potato and carrot mash but it's your choice but by using carrot to bulk up the mash you are saving calories. If you do use white potatoes, make sure you only have the same combined weight. This mash also freezes well so you might consider making bigger batches for convenience.

Serves 1 - 325 calories
***Mash is suitable for freezing
Preparation - 10 minutes
Cooking - 20 minutes

- 1 tuna steak approx 125g / 4½ oz each
- 1 sweet potato - 200g / 7 oz peeled weight
- 1 medium carrot
- 1 medium tomato
- 100g / 4 oz of Broccoli florets
- 1 garlic clove

Method

Peel and chop sweet potato into largish chunks and the carrots into smaller slices as they take longer to cook. Boil in lightly salted water until soft, about 10-15 minutes depending on size, then mash with a little seasoning but no butter.

Oven bake the tuna sprayed with oil and water mixture for about 20 minutes or if you prefer, griddle for about 10 minutes turning over half way through cooking. Cut the tomato in half and place in another dish. Peel and slice the garlic and poke the slivers into the flesh of the tomatoes. Drizzle with a tiny amount of olive oil and some freshly ground pepper and bake for about 15 minutes.

Steam or microwave the broccoli as liked and serve with the tuna, mash and baked tomatoes.

Tuna Steak & Vegetables – 385 kcal

Serves 1 - 385 calories
Preparation - 10 minutes
Cooking - 25 - 30 minutes

- x 125g / 4½ oz Tuna Streaks
- 1 small onion
- 1 small parsnip
- 1 medium carrot
- ½ of small butternut squash
- 1 clove of garlic
- ½ x 400g / 14 oz tin of gluten-free chickpeas
- 1 tsp olive oil
- Juice of ½ lime
- 100ml / 3½ fl oz / scant ½ cup of water
- Small handful basil leaves

Method

Preheat the oven to 200°C/gas mark 6.

Peel and chop the onions, parsnips and carrots into bite sized pieces, not too big or they won't cook. Peel and slice the garlic and drain and rinse the chickpeas. Heat the oil in a large roasting dish in the pre-heated oven. While the oil is heating up, chop, de-seed and peel the squash, cutting it into 2-cm chunks.

Add the onions, parsnips, carrots and garlic to the roasting dish, stir to coat them in the oil and spread them out. Bake for 10 minutes. Then add the squash, together with the lime juice and mix well.

Roast for a further 15 minutes and then add the drained chickpeas and the water. Continue cooking for a further 10 minutes and then stir in the basil leaves.

During the final 10 minutes cooking time cook the tuna steak according to how you like it over a medium heat on a griddle or frying pan brushed very lightly with oil.

Put a portion of the roasted vegetables on each plate, topped by the tuna steak and serve with a green salad.

MEAT & POULTRY

Beef and Courgette Bake – 320 kcal

This dish uses courgette and tomatoes in place of high calorie potatoes for a type of cottage pie or lasagne. Freezes well so you can have it another day but will feed the whole family. Serve with some steamed vegetables and for the non fasting family members add some new potatoes or some crusty bread.

serves 4 – 320 calories per serving
***Suitable for freezing
Preparation – 10 minutes
Cooking – 60-70 minutes

- 350g/12oz low fat minced or ground beef
- 1 large onion

- 1 tsp dried mixed herbs
- 1 tbsp gluten-free flour
- 300ml or ½ pint or 1¼ cups gluten-free beef stock
- 1 tbsp gluten-free tomato puree
- 2 large tomatoes
- 4 medium courgettes or zucchini
- 2 tbsp cornflour
- 300ml or ½ pint or 1¼ cups skimmed milk
- 150ml or 5 fl oz or ⅔ cup low-fat fromage frais
- 1 egg yolk
- 4 tbsp grated parmesan cheese
- salt and pepper

Method

Pre-heat the oven to 190°C or 375°F or Gas 5

Finely chop the onion and thinly slice the tomatoes and courgettes.

Fry the beef and onion without any added oil for 5 minutes until browned all over. Drain off any surplus fat and then stir in the dried herbs, flour, stock and tomato paste and bring to a simmer. Cook for 30 minutes until the mixture is sauce like.

Transfer to an oven-proof dish relative to the portion you will be eating. Cover with a layer of sliced tomatoes and then courgettes. Leave to one side.

Mix the cornflour with a little of the milk to form a paste. Heat the remaining milk in either a saucepan or the microwave until just coming up to boil.

Add the cornflour paste and whip until it thickens and either stir over the heat for 1-2 minutes or pop back in the microwave for another minute. Remove from heat and beat in the fromage frais and the egg yolk.

Cover the layers of the meat dish with the white sauce, sprinkle with the grated parmesan cheese and bake in the oven for 25-30 minutes or until crisp and golden on top.

Chicken Lasagne – 390 kcal

An easy dish to cook for a dinner or late supper and it is very filling. It also uses up any leftover chicken.

serves 2 - 390 calories per serving
***Suitable for freezing
Preparation - 15 minutes
Cooking - 50-60 minutes

- 175g/6oz frozen chopped spinach thawed
- 200g/7oz cooked chicken
- 2 sheets no pre-cook gluten-free lasagne
- 3 tsp cornflour
- 220ml/8 fl oz/1 cup skimmed milk
- 2 tbsp parmesan cheese grated
- 200g / 7oz can chopped tomatoes
- 1 small onion
- 1 garlic clove
- 75ml / 2½ fl oz / ⅓ cup white wine

- 1½ tbsp gluten-free tomato puree
- 1 tsp dried tarragon

Method

Chop the cooked chicken and finely chop the onion and garlic clove. Make the tomato sauce by heating the tomatoes, onion, garlic, wine, tomato paste and dried tarragon in a pan. Bring to a simmer and cook for 20 minutes until nice and thick.

Season with salt and pepper and set aside.

Meanwhile, make sure the spinach is well drained and if necessary place on kitchen paper and mop until most of the water had gone.

Put the spinach into a suitable sized baking dish, one that will take the 2 sheets of lasagne in a single layer and season well. Cover the spinach with the cooked chicken and then the tomato sauce. Place the sheets of lasagne on top of this.

Make a white sauce by mixing the cornflour with a little of the milk and then add the rest of the milk to the paste. Heat either in a small saucepan for 2-3 minutes or in the microwave until the sauce is thick but not solid.

Cover the lasagne sheets with the white sauce, sprinkle the grated parmesan on top and bake for 25 minutes at 200C/400F/Gas 6 until the top is golden and bubbling. Serve with a green salad.

Although this recipe is really easy to do, I actually double up the ingredients, make two or four meals and freeze the excess. Less work all round and I always have a standby in the freezer for lazy fasting days.

Chicken and Chips – 400 kcal

You can't usually have this type of meal on your fasting days but this is a low fat version that just about creeps into your allowance.

serves 1 - 400 calories
Preparation - 10 minutes
Cooking - 30-35 minutes

- 1 x 225g/8 oz baking potato
- ½ tbsp sunflower oil
- 1 tsp coarse sea salt
- 2 tsp gluten-free plain flour
- ½ tsp paprika pepper
- 2 chicken drumsticks, no skin
- 1 small egg
- 1 tbsp water
- 1½ tbsp dry white gluten-free breadcrumbs

Method

Pre-heat oven to 200°C / 400°F / Gas 6

Scrub the potato but do not peel and cut into 8 equal size wedges. Put into a bowl with the oil and toss well to coat all over. Put on a non stick baking sheet or tray, sprinkle with the sea salt.

In a bowl, mix the flour with the paprika and season well. Coat the chicken with the flour mixture and shake off any excess. Beat the egg with the water and pour onto a plate. On another plate spread out the breadcrumbs. Now dip the chicken into the egg and then the breadcrumbs, making sure you cover as much chicken as you can.

Place the chicken on another non stick tray and bake in the pre-heated oven, together with the potato wedges for 30-35 minutes, turning the chicken after 15 minutes.

When cooked and crispy, drain the potato wedges onto kitchen paper to remove excess oil and serve with the chicken and perhaps a spoonful of low fat relish of choice.

Chicken & Wild/Brown Rice – 350 kcal

I love to cook a one pot dish because it is easier and saves on washing up. This dish is also very filling and nutritious because of the brown rice.

serves 2 - 350 calories per serving
***Suitable for freezing
Preparation - 5 minutes
Cooking - 45-50 minutes

- 1 medium onion
- 1 garlic clove
- 1 stick of celery
- 1 carrot
- 150ml / 5 fl oz / scant ¾ cup gluten-free chicken stock
- 175g/6oz skinless chicken breasts
- 110g / 4 oz mixed brown and wild rice
- 200g / 7 oz can chopped tomatoes
- 1 medium courgette/zucchini

Method

Chop the onion, crush the garlic, slice the celery, dice the carrot and thinly slice the courgette.

Put the onion, garlic, celery and carrot in a large pan with the stock, bring to a simmer, cover and cook on a low heat for 5 minutes.

Cut the chicken into 2.5cm/ 1 inch cubes and add to the pan. Stir and cover again and cook for a further 5 minutes.

Add the rice and chopped tomatoes, season, bring back to the boil, cover and simmer gently for 25 minutes.

Stir in the sliced courgettes and carry on cooking for another 10 minutes but without the lid. Stir occasionally to prevent sticking, adding more water if it is getting too dry and the rice has not fully cooked. Serve with a green salad.

Italian Turkey Steak – 325 kcal

Turkey is one of the cheapest cuts of meat and really low in fat content so make the most of this with an easy to cook meal. Because you are having new potatoes, you won't realise this is a fasting day.

Serves 2 – 325 calories per serving
Preparation – 10 minutes
Cooking – 15-20 minutes

- 2 turkey steak fillets
- 225g / 8 oz small new potatoes
- 115g / 4oz runner beans
- 1 tbsp gluten-free pesto sauce
- 2 tbsp olive oil
- Juice and zest of ½ lemon
- 1 garlic clove
- 2 medium tomatoes

Method

Trim and thickly slice the runner beans. De-seed and chop the tomatoes into chunks. Crush the garlic. Cook the new potatoes for 8 minutes, add the runner beans and cook for another 4 minutes.

While the potatoes and beans are cooking, make a few shallow cuts into each side of the turkey fillet and press the pesto sauce onto both sides of the turkey. Heat 1 tbsp oil in a large non-stick frying pan and cook the turkey for 3-4 minutes each side until they start to go brown. Sprinkle with the lemon juice and zest and cook to reduce. Remove from the pan and keep hot.

Drain the vegetables and heat the remaining olive oil in the pan. When the oil is warm, stir in the potatoes, beans, garlic and tomatoes and cook for about 2 minutes. Serve with the turkey steaks and the liquid from the pan.

Honey Chicken with Pasta – 365 kcal

This is ideal for a barbecue or summer buffet because it can be eaten hot or cold. The pasta pushes up the calories a bit so try having just a salad or steamed broccoli if you are near your limit and deduct 150 calories.

serves 1 - 365 calories per serving
Preparation - 10 minutes
Cooking - 20-25 minutes

- 1 x 125g/4oz boneless chicken breast
- 1 tsp clear honey
- 1 tsp soy sauce
- ½ tsp grated lemon rind
- 1 tsp lemon juice
- salt and pepper
- 45g / 1 ¾ oz gluten-free very small size pasta
- 3 cherry tomatoes

- 1 tsp olive oil
- 1 pinch chilli flakes

Method

Preheat the grill to medium

Skin the chicken and trim off any fat. Pat dry and score a criss-cross pattern on both sides of the breast but make sure you do not cut all the way through.

In a small bowl, mix the honey, soy sauce, lemon rind and juice and plenty of seasoning.

Put the chicken on the grill or barbecue rack and brush with half of the honey glaze. Cook for 10 minutes, turn the chicken over and brush with the rest of the glaze. Cook for another 10 minutes or until cooked through, depending on your barbecue heat.

While the chicken is grilling, cook the pasta according to the packet instructions, drain and mix in the olive oil and chilli flakes and season with black pepper and salt and keep warm.

Serve the pasta with the cooked chicken, halved cherry tomatoes some extra lemon zest and a green salad or steamed broccoli.

Lamb Kebabs - 325 kcal

Serves 1 - Calories approximately 325 per serving
Preparation 10 minutes
Cooking - 15-25 minutes

- 200g / 7 oz lean lamb steaks
- ½ red pepper
- ½ green pepper
- 25g / 1 oz low-fat yoghurt
- 1 tsp olive oil
- 1 small onion
- several fresh sprigs of rosemary

Method

Cut the lamb into 2-cm cubes, removing any excess fat. Put the cubes into a bowl; pour over the yogurt and olive oil. Toss in the mixture making sure the lamb is fully covered. Cover and chill for at least 4 hours or overnight if you have time.

When ready, remove lamb from fridge, peel and cut the onion into quarters, chop the peppers into cubes and thread onto the skewers alternating lamb, peppers and onion. Metal skewers are fine but if using bamboo you should soak them first to avoid burning and the food sticking.

Cook them on a hot barbecue or under a pre-heated grill, laying them on a piece of foil and a few fresh sprigs of rosemary, until they are done to your taste.

Serve with a green salad and low calorie tzatsiki as a dressing.

Sausages in Batter - 325 kcal

This is a low fat version of Toad in the Hole. You can get low fat gluten free sausages in good supermarkets or on line.

Serves 2 - 325 calories per serving
Preparation 10 minutes
Cooking – 55-60 minutes

- ½ red onion
- 4 low fat gluten-free sausages
- 1 tsp olive oil
- 50g / 2oz gluten-free plain flour
- 1 medium egg
- 150ml / 5 fl oz / scant ¾ cup skimmed milk
- 1 tsp gluten-free creamed horseradish
- 150g / 5 oz broccoli
- 100g / 4 oz carrots

Method

Pre-heat the oven to 200°C / Gas 6

Cut the onion into wedges and separate the layers. Place in a small shallow non-stick tin or ceramic dish. Arrange the sausages on top of the onions, add the oil and roast for 20 minutes.

Meanwhile make the batter by beating the egg into the sifted flour and then add the milk a little at a time until all the lumps have gone and the batter is nice and smooth.

Stir in the horseradish and season to taste. When the sausages have been cooking for the 20 minutes, pour the batter into the pan and put back in the oven for another 40 minutes until golden and fluffy. Serve with the steamed broccoli and carrots.

Marinated Balsamic Beef – 330 kcal

Use rump steak for this dish as it is fairly inexpensive especially if you can get it on offer. You could use cheaper cuts but I don't like chewy meat so would rather pay a little extra.

Serves 2 – 330 calories per serving
Preparation – 25 minutes (including marinating)
Cooking – 15-20 minutes

- 300g/13oz piece of rump streak
- 2 shallots
- 1 tbsp balsamic vinegar
- 250g/10oz new potatoes
- 125g / 4½ oz fresh washed spinach
- 1 tbsp olive oil

Method

Place the beef in a shallow tray or dish. Finely chop the shallots and mix with the balsamic vinegar. Rub this all over the meat and marinate for 20 minutes.

Wash the potatoes and thickly slice. Cook in salted boiling water for 12-15 minutes or until just tender and remove from the heat. Pop the spinach into the pan for a couple of minutes to wilt and then drain well and pour in the olive oil and some salt and pepper. Keep warm.

While the potatoes are cooking, grill or barbecue the marinated beef for 3-4 minutes each side depending on the thickness of the meat and your preference. Cook for longer if liked. Remove and wrap in foil for 5 minutes.

Slice the beef thinly across the grain and served on a bed of the potatoes and spinach. Sprinkle with a little balsamic vinegar and olive oil.

Pork and Plum Hotpot – 350 kcal

This is delicious especially when plums are in season and sweet and inexpensive.

serves 4 – 350 calories per serving
***Suitable for freezing
Preparation 10 minutes
Cooking – 35 – 40 minutes

- 400g / 14oz pork fillet
- 1 tbsp oil
- 1 garlic clove
- 175g / 6oz shallots
- 225g / 8oz plums
- 450ml / 15 fl oz / scant 2 cups gluten-free chicken stock
- 50g / 2 oz of gluten-free small size pasta

Method

Halve the shallots, crush the garlic, halve and stone the plums, if large halve again.

Cut the pork into 2.5cm/1 inch pieces and in a large frying pan, fry the meat and the garlic and shallots until browned all over.

Stir in the plums and stock, bring to the boil and simmer for about 10 minutes then add the pasta and cook for a further 10 minutes until the meat is cooked through and the pasta is soft. Add more stock if goes too dry before pasta is cooked.

Serve with a green salad and on a non fasting day some crusty bread.

Pork Stroganoff with Rice – 330 kcal

Use tender pork fillet to make this quick but delicious dish. The mushrooms and green pepper blend well with the tomato and yogurt sauce. If you eat it without the rice the calorie count drops to 195

Serves 2 – 330 calories per serving
***Suitable for freezing
Preparation - 10 minutes
Cooking - 30 minutes

- 175g / 6 oz lean pork fillet
- 1 tbsp vegetable oil
- 1 small onion
- 1 garlic clove – crushed
- 15g / ½ oz gluten-free plain flour
- 1 tbsp gluten-free tomato puree
- 225g / 7½ fl oz / 1 cup of gluten-free chicken or vegetable stock

- 75g / 3 oz button mushrooms
- 1 medium green bell pepper
- ½ tsp ground nutmeg
- 2 tbsp low-fat natural yogurt

To serve
- 75g / 3 oz basmati rice
- tbsp natural yogurt

Method

Chop the onion, slice the mushrooms and deseed and dice the green pepper. Trim the meat of all fat and skin and cut into 1cm or ½ inch slices.

Heat a large pan, add the oil and fry the pork, garlic and onion for 5 minutes until meat is slightly browned. Add the flour and tomato paste and stir through, then add the stock, a little at a time and mix well. Add the mushrooms, pepper, seasoning and nutmeg, bring back to the boil and simmer on a low heat for about 20 minutes.

Meanwhile cook the rice in a pan of boiling water for about 12 minutes or as directed on the packet. Drain and keep warm. Remove the Stroganoff from the heat, stir in the yogurt and serve with the rice in warmed bowls.

Tomato & Chicken with Pasta 340 kcal

This is a simple and economical pasta dish that will leave you full as well as happy. Cook enough of the sauce to freeze for another fasting day; just don't cook the pasta until needed.

Serves 4 – 340 calories per serving
***Suitable for freezing
Preparation – 5 minutes
Cooking – 30 minutes

- 3 tsp olive oil
- 4 boneless and skinless chicken breasts
- 1 medium onion
- 1 small courgette
- 2 cloves garlic
- 125ml / 4 fl oz / ½ cup gluten-free chicken stock
- pinch chilli flakes
- 400g / 14 oz can chopped tomatoes

- 125g / 4½ oz dry weight any gluten-free pasta

Method

Halve and finely slice the onion, courgette and garlic. Slice the chicken into long strips.

In a large pan heat 2 tsp olive oil and sauté the chicken until browned all over and remove from pan. Heat the remaining olive oil and add the onion, courgette, garlic and chilli flakes and cook for about 5 minutes.

Add the tomatoes and stock to the pan and return the chicken. Season well and simmer for a further 10 minutes. While the sauce is simmering, cook the pasta according to the pack and serve with the chicken.

About the Author

Liz Armond lives near London, England and is the author of numerous books, including an entire series designed specifically for followers of the 5:2 fast Diet. She started intermittent fasting as a way to manage her weight and when she discovered the 5:2 Fast Diet, it changed her life.

She is married, has two children 4 chickens and a cat. She is a keen golfer, rambler, and loves to ski whenever possible.

Please visit her website and blog for more up-to-date information

website:-   www.lizarmond.com
twitter:-   https://twitter.com/Liz_Armond
facebook:-   https://www.facebook.com/liz.armond

One Final Thing

If you believe the book is worth sharing, would you please take a few seconds to let your friends know about it on FaceBook and/or Twitter. If it turns out to make a difference in their lives, they'll be grateful.

All the best and good luck with your weight loss and I hope this diet changes your life as much as it did mine.

Liz Armond

Books by Liz Armond

Recipes for the 5:2 Fast Diet
Vegetarian for the 5:2 Fast Diet
Vegetarian & Gluten Free for the 5:2 Fast Diet
Gluten Free for the 5:2 Fast Diet
5:2 Diet Meal Plans &Recipes
Vegetarian Meal Plans for the 5:2 Diet
Breakfasts for the 5:2 Fast Diet
5:2 Diet Meals for One Cookbook
Vegetarian Meals for One for the 5:2 Diet
plus
Fasting Your Way to Health
Mediation for Beginners

DISCLAIMER AND/OR LEGAL NOTICES:

Every effort has been made to accurately represent this book and it's potential. Results vary with every individual, and your results may or may not be different from those depicted.

No promises, guarantees or warranties, whether stated or implied, have been made that you will produce any specific result from this book. Your efforts are individual and unique, and may vary from those shown. Your success depends on your efforts, background and motivation.

The material in this publication is provided for educational and informational purposes only and is not intended as medical advice.

The information contained in this book should not be used to diagnose or treat any illness, metabolic disorder, disease or health problem.

Always consult your physician or health care provider before beginning any nutrition or exercise program. Use of the programs, advice, and information contained in this book is at the sole choice and risk of the reader

NOTES

NOTES

NOTES

Printed in Great Britain
by Amazon